AF222366

EL-TAHRIR
LIBERATION SQUARE

The Arabian spring a decade later
2013–2023

N McNally

1st Edition, 2024

ISBN: 978-3-7597-0538-9

Publisher: BoD • Books on Demand GmbH, In de Tarpen 42, 22848 Norderstedt
Print: Libri Plureos GmbH, Friedensallee 273, 22763 Hamburg
Editor: N McNally

EL-TAHRIR
LIBERATION SQUARE

The Arabian spring a decade later
2013–2023

N McNally

INTERLUDE

Once settled at the table which would differ in shape and material due to the various cafes I regularly visited, space got made for the first newspaper to be unfolded carefully upon the wooden, metal or stone surface also withholding my cup of coffee, a glass of water and depending on the time of the day, the cherished croissant.

Through the procedure of reading, sipping and reading, turning page after page would I eventually come across information covering events or incidents which had taken place in north Africa. First the information dealt with governmental orders, new created legislations, direct decrees from the head person of those states, which mostly startled me as cruel and irrespective towards the people of those countries. I imagined the inhabitants weren't as well off and living in surroundings comparable to the people of western European countries.

From descriptions and stories on the previous pages of the newspaper, Frenchmen, Englishmen and Germans as well as Swiss financial commentators and especially Dutch folk would merely point out that more or less the whole of Africa was the third world. Meaning by living standards the African continent was equivalent to Gypsy Sinti shanty towns on the fringe of their own European Union. North Africans didn't have access to education, jobs, freedom of expression, democracy, travel rights and basic political involvement. Exactly like the Gypsy's in the eastern part of the European union including also a few countries in the western part. And if you are poor in the west of the European Union you may have access but too very low quality of everything.

So, for maybe some years these stories would repeat themselves. People weren't allowed to gather to talk about something that concerned them. Universities got closed. Criticism towards government became a criminal offence. A fish vendor got thrown into a dustbin lorry along with his stock of fish because he didn't have a authoriziation. People began to ignite themselves with petrol. Taxes rose whilst border crossings shut for security reasons. Religious minorities in the mostly diverse populations came under pressure after responsible figures of the states would pose alongside leading personalities of the main dominant religous belief. State and clerics side by side in front of a palace interior that bore the splendour of a rich environment. Not far from the sealed couple either to their flanks or strongly lingering in the background where faces of moustached men with sunglasses dressed in earth tone coloured suits. The decorated generals of this and that state force and sometimes they would inform the people of a city, town or village what time they expected them to be at home for dinner. The people also got reminded due to the events on the previous evening not to forget anything for their dinners or they wouldn't return home if they did and had gone out again to search for it. Meaning they could get assasinated. The handlings of people assemblies willing to express their discontent about regulations of their collective goods and the embedded possibilities of ascensions withheld within, which could lead towards the first world were confronted with deadly actions by police and military forces geared up in equipment provided by the first world.

Me sitting in the first world at a table sipping a watery coffee and going through a number of different newspapers, reaching the same conclusion every time after being confronted with the sports sector of the disclosing newspaper, that how long would the people of north Africa and deeper back in my mind, the people of the first world bear patronization by obviously corrupted establishments that showed the least of interest in even distribution of wealth and education. In the meantime, in these cafes I hardly ever came into conversation with present people touching these stories while I sat at my table turning the pages filled with news flanked by other tables. There was just no co-partner to comment on what had been written.

People around me didn't really speak much about topics circulating in newspapers. But when someone did, he or she, mostly a he would banter on against a group of people in our region, disregarding them the right to free speech and expression and it was only wright that the police handled them severely and heavily for doing so. Then followed the final comment which was more so a question over the observation, that, who was going to pay for the whole mayhem caused? Shortly afterwards the newspapers would then inform that the local parliament had come up with new regulations on how their installed powers would in the future deal which such occurrences.

Over in north Africa parliaments had meanwhile altogether ceased to gather for discussions aiming to regulate further ongoing matters and future ones. Following the ever-growing assemblies of people and the spilling of blood in the efforts to discharge them, something was bound to change.

The people's assemblies continued.

The newspapers I was reading now, would cover the assemblies and inform on what had been discussed amongst the congregated people and what their desires were in terms of future regulations for themselves. To achieve their longings meant that the group of people or person who had neglected their involvement in the distribution of their collective goods and had sought to deprive and deteriorate their lives, would soon stand in court and face justice or run to hide in a remote desert town or village most desirably never to return again.

Soon means in a short space of time but the newspapers repeatedly reported on more lethal street violence between stone throwing people occasionally additionally refurbished with Molotov cocktails against masses of stick and shield wielding policemen backed by colleagues distributing various gases and live ammunition.

Every now and then similar scenes just without live ammunition but instead with rubber bullets had and would still erupt close by my café table or in distance cities in the realms of the European Union. Discontent people expressing themselves over new regulations that would neglect and disrespect their livelihoods and environments. Which then in the first world at some stage of the event could turn violent and the police more or less easily by sheer strength and equipment would joyfully deal with the situation. Resistance from the people had little chance of success. Condemnation of the event was sure to follow in the next days morning newspaper. Violence from the people was wrong and it denied them their reason for being discontent. Violence from the police was tolerated and necessary to protect city streets from being filled to long with angry people claiming things.

Not so in north Africa. People remained in the streets day after day and challenged the police forces to stand their ground for their future regulations and beliefs. The people had voices in newspapers who echoed their demands and condemned the brutal police violence.

Only until concealment orders were issued against newspapers by the opposing figures in the chief positions of the state and the journalistic landscape dried up.

But their powers and forces couldn't reach out to silence the European newspapers who continued to cover the peoples demands for freedom of speech and expression, political involvement and democracy for all citizens.

The further cases of access to education and the respect of diversity including the equal distribution of goods and wealth were missing a centre place in the narrative and created picture. Too great were the blazing street fires which in some cases licked the windows of government buildings till the pressure let them burst and the flames danced through to spend the night within. By the time day had dawned and past noon time, heads of states had fled the palaces and left the country or had got put under arrest with the prospect of getting trialled before a high court.

The people's assemblies continued.

Democratic elections were scheduled with the support of the European Union. The people celebrated their achievements gained through their fearless persistence of assembling and chanting their demands to the spirits of the interweaving winds.

To me sitting in or outside the café or at home on my sofa reading the newspaper, it seemed like the Arab spring, the uprising of people had led to a revolution which would bring change and create a path for the majority of people to ascend towards the first world. Corruption was over, education could at last be free and mutual respect would be granted to everyone. The people just had to rearrange in parliament, summon their views and desires, vote their politicians and the better just lay around the corner. That's how the situation looked like when I reached the sports sector of the newspaper. My conclusion now was an altercation had been achieved and wouldn't it be interesting to hear from the people on first hand how they had endured the governmental hostility and accomplished their common visions.

Unmediated information is surely valuable and withholds the quality of true guidance against forces of opposition to one's visions and common goals.

Egypt's people had to endure a terrible corrupt puppet master for a long period in a person's lifetime and had finally overthrown him with the help of the military, now voted into power in the country's first democratic election, a man called Mohammed Morsi from the Muslim brotherhood.

The newspaper I'm reading now is reporting of new discontent, but to me its not clear from which source of power it is arising and Mr. Morsi isn't even 100 days in power as democratic elected president.

CHAPTER 1

Parallel to daily life in Egypt unfolding itself newly morning after morning informative events covering Egypt's recent turmoil were being held in my Swiss town. The series of events was titled: What do the revolutions of the Arab spring mean for Europe?

These events were being organised by the federal bureau of foreign affairs.

What more could I want for preparation to my still in the shape of an idea adventure. The people invited to talk on the panels of these events were either inhabitants of the affected regions such as the likes of journalists or book authors or employees from diplomacy corps and intellectuals who were familiar with north Africa. The panels got moderated and the evenings would give insight to what had been developing and had happened in north Africa, what possibilities could the future bear for the regions and its people. Being introduced to some north African book authors I only found it wright and proper to purchase a book or two for further assimilation. Such as Nagib Machfu's book *Young Cairo* and Susanne Schanda's book, *Literatur der Rebellion*.

Beside all the talk of what and how things had happened especially in Cairo, a lady informed us on special public action which was just being organised for the very first time in Egypt's modern history. A people's petition had been lanced, which the initiators called Tamarod and it would last till the 30th of June 2013.

In detail the petition required the resignation of President Morsi. This meant as many people as wished to could sign up till the end of June. By then a clear number of participants was the result which withheld a precise will factor of the people of Egypt. Their voice as just recently had thundered through the foundations of the capital was surely to be unmistakably heard yet another time by the compatriots of power. I noted the name of the petition in my notebook, greatly thanked the speakers on the panel and stepped out into the cold wintery night air of February.

Not for long did Egypt remain in my mind with Tamarod left as a word in my notebook. Meanwhile I slowly became aware that going to Egypt didn't seem like a place to go to for a young Swiss man who had a girlfriend who regularly went to Paris to live on the "Les grand boulevards". There was nobody from my group of friends I could think of who could join me. Just telling someone of my idea would startle the person who then pointed out what had previously taken place in Egypt further inquiring about the present security situation. Listening to the anxious person didn't feel to inviting in telling them about me wanting to gain first hand information on how to topple a corrupt government, let alone a possible chance in exercising and enlarging one's knowledge in street combat. Nobody around me expressed their compassion for distance suppressed people, not even for the surpressed people in the first world.

So, quickly did I realise that my idea would just be my idea and most likely stay my idea. But to divert the anxiety of the listener I came up with a new idea which sounded more comprehensible while equally adventurous.

Even I had to say to myself, that it promised a great experience if it happened as I imagined it could.

First, Egypt had two famous holiday destinations. Sharm el-sheik was the first but isn't on Egyptian mainland and didn't fit into my motion picture. The second place reasonably did fit and is called Hurgada. It lay between the red sea and the great river Nile and most people know it as a cheap holiday site. The red sea sounded very inviting to me also because of the prospect of me being able to tan up so I could mix in with the locals who surely weren't as pale as I was. Then once satisfied with splashing about in the sea and roasting in the sand could well exist the possibility of sailing or traveling down the Nile into Cairo. That sounded to like a common holiday idea for a Swiss bloke, playing football in a local club and going out with a dentist's daughter. Everyone who asked me what I was doing on my summer holidays, remember holidays are a main subject in first world life, was going to receive as an answer, Hurgada to Cairo on the Nile and my summer holidays were beginning on the 30th of June.

A flight to Hurgada with a cheap suite bedroom plus all-inclusive was easily found in the internet which I booked a month prior to the end of June. Finally had I the basics organised and an adventure of a very different kind to me lay ahead. As a child I heard distant explosions, was checked at gunpoint at military checkpoints. As a young teenager I have been to Amsterdam and got charged down by horse ridding policemen yielding very long batons, sited green German police tanks coming my way, sniffed a bit of tear gas, dodged jets of water from water cannons and also felt them, but going to Cairo seemed like sailing out into the blue and I hadn't even considered consciously the problems I would have arising from the to me totally foreign language spoken in Eygpt.

CHAPTER 2

Week after week passed in its daily routine and finished on the yearned for Friday. Up at the same time every morning, football training every second evening, guys competing for a place in the starting eleven on the weekend. Everyone had equal chances. One's effort and commitment counted. Not quite true because a couple of the players had an unofficial fixed position. But none the less masculine dominance was in the air from the beginning of the gathering till the end around the lager beer tables. Worldly subjects, not a word heard or spoken. New shoes new this, party there, you're a twat, he's a leek, she's like that. All right all right I did my best, gave the effort but also here the routine dabs out the light and ones lightness. Top down from the coach favourism. I remember there are exceptions.

Back home with my girlfriend. I'm having a Minestrone for dinner, it's 22:30 o'clock. She has eaten already. My roommate and her are having a jolly time in front of the telly while I eat and look at them lying on the sofas. All I hear is commentary. In my room.

She's getting on but our senses aren't tickled by one another and I haven't yet come to realise the structure in my football team to share my thoughts about it with her. We aren't talking much really. A few bits from our day, then some minutes of play, on our backs we lay, a kiss good night. Sleep well. My mind fixes my situation, traces back the days and weeks. I wonder if our relationship is full of love but shouldn't I be feeling more of it crosses through my mind as I end up thinking that my withdrawal to Egypt will certainly show what I feel I am missing. I have informed her of the backdrop of my travel intentions and by her response I acknowledge that she can't quite relate to my interest although she has just been recently traveling through parts of India.

So, after all its all down to me and solely for me. Thanks to a friend and his family was I able to contact his aunt who permanently lives in Cairo and she declared herself willing to host me if I eventually showed up.

Weeks of semi waiting have passed. I was content with my organising and very enjoyable did I find the Egyptian literature which I have meanwhile read. Standing in my cellar compartment a tricky moment starts to get a grip of me as I look over my choice of traveling bags. A rucksack type bag must definitely be used because I have to be able to move with vacant hands. Necessarily even be able to run with it on. I have three types to choose from. One of them is too small because I have scheduled three weeks for my excursion. Blue and black Mammut Tramp backpack or a green greyish Californian travel bag convertible from rucksack to suitcase? Somewhere is also a label stuck prominently on it bearing the Stars and Stripes. I consider the heat in Egypt and my moving from place to place. Eventually I decide to take the Californian bag due to its functional interior and neat layout.

Back upstairs in my room I pile out what I think I will really need. My imagination sways off to Egypt and how the average male dresses himself. According to my thoughts I choose in regard to that criteria. Long trousers but surely not jeans. Simple cotton t-shirts and shirts. One jumper for cold desert nights. Swimming trunks and towels and finally my practical small sleeping bag. The Californian bag manages my garments perfectly as I lean it upright against my bed to inspect its full appearance. Suddenly a flow of challenging thoughts swirl around in my mind as I figure out the possibility of being an American spy or an European journalist in the eye and mind of Egyptian authorities as I will enter their circles of observation and control. My freedom and life will be at stake with that Californian rucksack. A couple of gruesome stories about captured, tortured and then killed westerners had been published in the newspapers I had recently read. With these images in my head I sternly decided to unpack my green greyish convertible rucksack and abandon it for another sort of journey. The black and blue Mammut Mountain climber bag would surely leave a more disinterring impression on a person with anti -western sentiment. I wasn't at all keen on exercising any sort of prison visit. From what I had read about Egyptian internment, it sounded like middle age dungeons administered with a scrupulous indifference.

I couldn't see any harm in swapping my bag and rightly my intention was for my safety and fortune. The Mammut bag took over the luggage situation and the image of a western intruder departed from my mind. Tranquillity regained position within myself as I test shouldered the bag.

My state of being remained in a calm gradual form only that I felt lightly teased on my nerves fringes by the fact that I was going to Africa. Meaning towards a whole new scenery guided by a spirit of weighty reasons but none the less stepping softly in a special embedded atmosphere.

The question most important to me was, could I gather enough impressions and information to benefit a colossal change in Europe and a long its outreaching tentacles. Boarding the aeroplane, feeling a bit unsteady, I found it well booked and my seat directly to Hurgada was next to a fleshy white male wearing black hard plastic sunglasses and a baseball cap. The man was in his mid-forties, American and on his way to Iraq via Oman. He asked if I was arabian then after learning not, did he mention his dislike for arabs. After telling him my reasons for flying to Egypt, the Nile tour trip obviously, he began opening up an insight into his recent life as a truck driver paid by American interests to transport crude Oil under violent and hostile circumstances. He operated in the shadows of the protection shield of the American military and their contractors such as the likes of Black Water Securities. His story went from desert tours in trucks to trucks smashing in prison walls to liberate convicted fellow Americans and other allies who were involved in robbery, kidnapping and brutal violence related to territory and turf fighting among themselves and local Iraqi's according to him. The truck driver made it very clear, he spoke harsh and threatening, that the attitude they lived by was "don't fuck with us Americans" and if you do, you'll find yourself in a terrible situation. By this time, I just had enough of his madness and tried to disconnect from his disrespectful stories. I even have in mind that he started to verbally molest an Arabian woman sitting in the same row as us. I intervened for peace in our row. The guy was a complete brut downing simultaneously alcoholic beverages. Thanks to our lunch arrival did the man shortly afterwards calm down. Looking out into the blue, beneath us lay the world, precise maybe Greece and the story of this one sitting next to me out thousands of employed men in war correlated shockingly to what I had read in newspapers in previous years.

What a world people are up against if they have to deal with hordes of men like this fellow sitting next to me. I know Yanks are mostly loud mouthed when on holidays but imagining them armed to the teeth and them thinking their still on a sort of holiday sweating out the alcohol and whatever else, day after day to maintain their Marshall posture, crying out loud, Iraq must be an nightmare for its inhabitants. Fine fine, nice talking to you and yes, I hope not too many people will come into harms way around you. He's sipping on a can of beer and going to catch a connecting flight further into the middle east.

Gosh, I think to myself, what did a human's life mean to that man?

Entering the luggage disposal of Hurgada airport I face more people I'm not familiar with. Hordes of Russians dressed in beach gear shuttle around me with their luggage trolleys making it unmistakably clear through their loud speaking that they are here and where they are exactly came from. Surprising similarities with the yanks. I gather my travel rucksack que at the boarder customs awaiting my entry and passport stamping to Egypt, not feeling nervous or anything equivalent. Just realising it's the same airport procedures as anywhere else. But at least here I have a hotel room waiting for me.

CHAPTER 3

As my turn arrives to face the Egyptian boarder officer nothing unorderly has occurred to me as my gaze followed the people granted free passage to the exit lying across the white marmot floor hall. So far no one had been stopped for longer inquiries. I face the officer whose uniform is as white as snow with a dark blue badge of rank with golden strips on each shoulder. The man is sitting and flanked by a second chap standing next to him. Both a wearing a black sort of rimed beret cap and sport neatly tended moustaches. All right I think to myself, I'm looking forward to splashing in your red sea and I´ve got a Hotel close by. Surely do I not classify for a foreign spy. I answer their questions politely. The man sitting brushes through the pages of my passport. Well it has quite a number of stamps ranging from various eastern European country's to Latin and north America.

The two officers begin to conversate with each other. After a short while into their to me non-understandable exchange of phrases does the man sitting order me to pass on through. I walk on relieved and at the exit I´m ordered to show my passport again to an officer. I present the entry stamp to him; he is also dressed like a sailor off to a ball night. He doesn't wave me onwards but instead orders a comrade to come over and have a look as well at my presented passport page. I'm asked to follow the one officer.

We walk back across the hall and come to a wooden door of an office with two chairs outside. The officer takes my passport and goes inside while I am ordered to sit down and wait. An hour passes by with no information coming through the door holding my passport. I stay calm and watch the flow of arriving passengers being checked and then disappearing through the exit door probably directly to their all-inclusive holiday bargain. Grossly hordes of pink Russians. If they want to send me back, they can I don't really care. The other thing that crosses my mind is, that how on earth am I going to communicate if the opposite person doesn't speak English. The Arab language is so totally unknown to me. At last the officer comes through the door holding my passport. In a tone of innocence, I ask the chap what had caused the delay. He first answers that because of the ongoing changes in the central bureaucracy in Cairo, due to the turmoil, was it not clear who had the overall say at the moment. I thought of the current tensions amongst peoples advocates and government forces. He the continued, saying that new was tugging with the old on all floors of power which reached out to all posts. I acted as not quite understanding what he was describing to finish our little conversation off looking for a reassuring answer from him that everything was fine for me now. The young officers turned his last answer towards my passport as he told me that I had received on entering the hall a departure stamp but now my passport was fitted with the correct required one for entering Egypt soundly. I thanked him uprightly for his partaking in the lengthy matter and as I turned on my heels to head for the exit, hopefully finally, I peered into the office as I passed by to see an elderly overweight moustache bearing sailor man who looked very authoritarian sitting at a desk chatting to a comrade. All these chaps would be taking orders from somewhere dawned on me, portraying the obvious from what I had just learnt from the junior officer and the peoples cause was challenging the erected governmental structures which I had depicted out of the newspapers and books. I left the air-conditioned hall and stepped outside to face a disclosing day in an apathetic air of heat walking and feeling not light footed at all.

CHAPTER 4

Shortly after I left the airport building, was I sitting in the back of taxi. I passed on the address of my hotel and hoped the driver would find it. Peering out the car window we passed concrete buildings in various sizes but mainly they were in rectangular form and erected next to tarmac roads. Dust and heat floated in the air whilst a yellowish grey set the tone of close and near. I think I remember the driver being able to speak some German but not much more than courtesy was exchanged between us. At last a familiar sight unfolded itself in a blink of an eye in front of me as the turquoise blue sea appeared at the bottom of the hill and stretched itself evenly into the sky with only the odd patch of white appearing small and irregularly amongst it. What I couldn't see from our higher situated position was a beach. The seafront didn't show itself anywhere and I could only guess where it lay by the last line of buildings stretched out along the coastline. My taxi turned sharply and headed in the direction of the sea where we came into an area made up by the looks of hotel buildings. Literally no one was walking about. Not for long did the taxi driver continue his smooth operation till he announced that we had arrived.

The building we had come to a halt in front of, was about eight stories high with balconies lining one side and below lay a swimming pool tucked away behind bushes and rows of palm trees. I payed and thanked the man and went inside. Conveniently a couple of minutes later was I accompanied to my room door where I was handed the keys and given some instructions referring to house safety in an emergency situation. I shut the door glanced approvingly at the huge elevated bed, put my black and blue mountain rucksack down on the suitcase holder acknowledging the rooms wealthy interior to step out afterwards onto the balcony. I must have been on the seventh floor. My view began on a dusty square which inhabited rusty construction material and one or two elderly trucks. A number of light brown dogs strayed about and no traffic was to be seen. It looked like the end of town or the end of the world. Beyond the close but last line of greyish yellow buildings and even so yellow hills rolled out into the growing dusk where peaks of distant purple sharp rocky mountains loomed through a screen of dust. Where on earth, was I clenched my heart and soul as I grasped for air realising that I was far away from anyone I loved or cherished. Why on earth was I all alone struck me full heartedly as I withdrew my gaze from the distant rocks and sand to stagger back inside the room where I collapsed on my bed and spread out in mourn and tears. My room appeared to me as cast away in a place I was totally disconnected from leaving me to answer why I was here at all and on top completely alone. Shouldn't you be with your girlfriend or be somewhere in Europe crossed my mind. Nothing was to be done except for letting my tears roll down my cheeks and cry till I didn't cry no more.

After a while I stopped crying and I realised that I had just had a sort of breakdown. I assured myself that the room I was in was in a hotel and the hotel was in Hurgada and Hurgada was in Egypt and I was standing wright in the middle of it. The room had meanwhile become dark.

Night had fallen and the sky withheld a wonderful warm lighted moon surround by the odd million bright shining stars.

I turned on the television to quickly halt on a channel showing a square in Cairo full of people chanting in chorus. Something was obviously boiling up in the capital. Shortly after watching my mind reconstructed my initial plans and I saw myself tanning by the seaside after breakfast the following morning.

I felt resolute and confident remembering that I had chose something else than usual and this me being in this room was it's beginning. Soon afterwards I fell into a deep sleep where I faced my girlfriend and other things of meaning. Nothing had the power to alternate this fact and principal.

Waking up the following morning my turbulences in heart had eased off and the nights sleep had refreshed my spirit and soul. Once again whole hearted I set out first for the breakfast table in the hotel to nourish myself, for the days main aim was to find a nice beach for sunbathing and swimming. Staff in my hotel told me roughly which other hotel I would have to find which would then grant me access to the beach but in return of a fee. On hearing this I felt a bit disgusted and wasn't quite prepared to believe what I had just heard. None the less I rolled up my beach towel, stuck it under my arm and off I went heading for the coastline. Over head a blue sky spread out with drifting patches of silk clouds in it. The heat seemed bearable probably because a light breeze ascended every now and then. Soon after walking for a couple of minutes did it become clear to me that where I was located wasn't really local residents Hurgada. Hardly anyone was outside with me on the pavements and the medium sized buildings were all hotels. After crossing a number of scarcely frequented streets I ended up on a square in front of a long sand coloured building which I assumed was the described place providing beach access. Unmistakably written over a spacious arch entry in the building was the word Beach Club. I halted a short distance away from the entrance keen to find out if there wasn't any other spot offering free beach access. Scanning my surrounding nothing convincing showed itself to me. Taxi after taxi pulled up on the square opposite the beach club producing a batch of people sharing my primary idea for the day. After walking up and down the building in search of a glimpse of the sea I reluctantly gave up finding the gap and stepped into the entry hall of the beach club. Once inside the airport like hall, it had ticket counters, could I at last see still a short distance away across a sandy beach the blue water spilling easily upon the shore. Straight ahead I calmly walked through the tiled room intending to reach the steps descending onto the beach. Thinking that luck most likely would be on my side because of the other men and women distracting the guards for their access to the beach had I dared to claim uprightly free pathway. It seemed too wrong having to pay to gain access to the seaside and no alternative was made available. Someone in the room began to shout and soon was I forced to realise that the uproar was directed at me. It wouldn't make sense to run out on to the beach so I turned around to address the vocal and uneased man.

And so, it was me who was causing the trouble. The man wanted to know from me why I wouldn't wait for my turn to which I just pointed at the sea. I uttered the word swim, swim but the man pointed towards the man behind the counter and clearly said pay that amount. I repeatedly pointed at the sea and said free but he wouldn´t have any of it. Showing astonishment, I gradually pulled out the required paper bills and passed them across the counter to the equally astonished man. I wasn't happy as I walked through the warm sand in search of a vacant deckchair. The beach park was lightly populated and a very orderly atmosphere crept amongst the people. Nothing comparable to Europe's beaches. The average male lying, walking or talking about was grossly overweight. There were maybe as many women in bikinis as there were in full skin covering bathing suits and to my now approved understanding why the guard had sceptically asked if I was alone when paying my entrance fee, hardly any single people were present amongst the pairs and families.

Glancing to my left then rightwards from my standing point in the main assembly of deckchairs centred in the middle of the beach park flanked by food and drink stalls did I hesitatingly make my way through all having spotted a vacant lying chair on the side where I could feel undisturbed and the other way around. The water wasn't that refreshing and either was the place itself. I spent a couple of hours trying to relax and imagining that I was enjoying myself but this beach club wasn't getting the better of me. The place seemed so superficial and unauthentic it was hard for me to bear. I wasn't used to this sort of exclusivity and longed for the proper local life which surely was flourishing somewhere. Come afternoon I set back to my hotel and asked where Hurgadas town centre was.

Once back outside the hotel my intention was to stop a mini van which I noticed was likely to be a collective taxi similar to the ones in Latin America. Likewise, I hadn't seen any white people use them but I knew it was down to me if I wanted to experience them.

I would quickly find out if I was welcome. Standing by the roadside a short distance away from my hotel I stuck out my arm as soon as I saw one of the vans approaching, traveling in the direction of Hurgada town.

The van stopped next to me, so I climbed in to sit on one of the three short benches amongst a handful of local men and women. No one seemed startled at me boarding so I felt I could relax for the first few moments. Slowly as we sped along to somewhere, did I recognise the feeling of arrival and inner comfort spread out within me. On route people hopped off and on and each person would pass on their travel fare to the person sitting in front, so it could end up in the hands of the co-driver. Up over a hill we drove from where we could see the turquoise blue sea and it became clear to me because of the change of buildings that we were entering local inhabitants Hurgada. The place looked like a quite coastal town with no splendour or any specific outstanding all overshadowing monuments or buildings. The co-driver eventually directed a question at me. I simply responded with "centre" to which he introduced his German language abilities due to his stay there in recent years.

I don't remember much of my time in the town, except that after spending some time sitting in a tea parlour drinking sweet mint tea that from a distance a noise began to arise which came closer and closer.

I soon made out that it must be coming from lots of people somewhere close by who were shouting words in choir. The men in the venue head for the door and so did I. Once outside a couple of dozen people appeared in a side road waving Egyptian flags and chanting the same phrase over and over again. Tailing behind the boisterous group a handful of policemen patrolled in pick up vehicles. The parade walked out onto the town centre roundabout in front of us and circled round it to then halt while a few participants held short speeches. Astonished by the event my conclusion was that the demonstration in front of me had to have something to do with yesterday nights events in

Cairo which I had seen briefly on television.

After the small demonstration dispersed which had called out for the removal of president Morsi from office, I had finished in the meantime a number of glasses of mint tea and I was mainly occupied with thinking of how to proceed in the up coming days. Slightly electrified I pondered over the masses of people that had gathered the previous night in Cairo and being now confronted with the equivalent here in Hurgada but on a much smaller scale. My eye had fixed the Egyptian eagle flying firmly on the many red white and black flags rippling above enchanted faces of men women and children. Considering my main reasons for being in Egypt and acknowledging simultaneously the distanced and disappointing impression Hurgada withheld in comparison to Cairo, well Cairo was the epicentre, it seemed reasonable to leave for the capital as soon as possible. Firstly though, would I have to get in contact with my friend's aunt Lisa who lived in Cairo and see if I was welcome on an earlier term as agreed. It was in the middle of the afternoon as I left the tea parlour in Al-Dohr in a taxi van destined for the hotel district. Back in my hotel room Lisa answered my telephone call and confirmed that Cairo surely was the place to be at the moment and I was absolutely welcome as soon as I could make it to her neighbourhood Agouza.

Not losing any time I set out again returning to the old town of Hurgada in search of the long-distance bus terminal which I assumed would sell bus tickets to Cairo.

Conveniently I purchased my ticket and the bus to Cairo was scheduled for lunch time the next day. Holding the key to the next part of my adventure I returned to my hotel walking a good part of the route in search of interesting places and direct sea front access. Unfortunately, none of my side interests were fulfillable so I stuck my arm out to an approaching taxi van hoping there was enough space for me. Later that night on prime time television military personal appeared declaring on the national news channel that they had agreed to give the elected president of their state 48 hours to quite his office.

In the months running up to this particular event basic necessities such as flour, cooking oil, gas and petrol aswell as other things had become rare which drove the prices up. Newspapers had suggested that these were reasons for the souring of the people. Some newspapers even suggested it was done deliberately. Which could well be when taking into account that the distributing companies belonged to the military holdings. One other reason of probability hadn't made it into the narrative of events and that was the petition of Tamarod. The signed will of the people. Summing things up, president Morsi wasn't good for relations with Israel or with its patron the USA, also was his party committed to humanitarian and social policies, but one other big factor of anguish was his muslim brotherhood foundation which frightened the secular state. Looking back in this instance, it seems like the military generals were hijacking the peoples petition in regard of maintaining the capitalist status quo on behalf of interests relating to western policies and global liberalism dogmas. The other obvious was that the mongrels didn't want another peoples revolution which Tamarod was holding in store. Tamarod meant a true democratic process was playing out and the state was there to fulfil it. The generals who now were confronting the nation and the nation knew quite well of the militarys huge seized apparatus with its connection into nearly every Egyptian family due to their role as employers. None the less, I wasn't aware of these issues at the time and only sought to support the forces searching for altercation of the status quo. I still couldn't understand any

Arabian but the hotels TV satellite produced half the worlds channels which were meanwhile all tuned into the events on Liberation square, the translation of Tahrir and explaining in languages which were familiar to me. The military portrayed themselves as supporters of the people and the president had two days to withdraw but of course it didn't seem fair after just 100 days in power.

CHAPTER 5

The next morning, I gave up visiting the beach club and decided to experience a couple of hours beside the hotels swimming pool. The suns strength was just the same as down on the beach and rarely had I hung out by a circler swimming pool as a hotel resident. Lunchtime arrived rather rapidly which meant I would have to buckle my packed mountain hiking rucksack and get into town to buy some provisions for the journey to Cairo. In a number of stores I summed up some local take away food and a litre or two of water. Being inwardly lightly nervous but outwardly reserved like a local dressed up in long cotton trousers and a linen long sleeved dark blue shirt I stood with the rest of the travellers patiently in line waiting to board the coach. I even carried two towels with me for inside in case the local travel culture would be Air Conditioning mad. In Latin America I had experienced sorry bus voyages in 14°degrees when outside it was something over 25°degrees. Real terror trips, so for the possibility the towels would be my response to such regulations. Who would want to arrive at their destination freezing and sick? Certainly not me. Going up the steps we generally all entered the bus in an anonymous attitude without greeting the personal. As I reached the third row of seats I chose to sit down.

A tall friendly, young looking man with short dark haired curls took up seat next to me and we quickly found out we could only communicate with each other by hand gestures. Punctually on time our vehicle rumbled into action leaving Hurgada's panorama behind us for yellow dry and stony hills with rising mountains on its horizon on one side with the red sea stretched out along thin stony strands on the other side. Every now and then huge concrete building shells appeared on the seafront side obscurely seldomly accomplished. But the buildings signalled that once finished thousands upon thousands of hotel beds would be available, if, was the question hanging over the bare impression. Some of the buildings didn't even have proper beaches. Strangely enough they were actually completely isolated in the vastness of sand, rock, dust and sea. Hours past and we occasionally halted for a brake. Outside the bus the heat was just about bearable in the shade of a tree and I didn't mind returning to the 19° degrees within the bus.

Five hours of journey had past and meanwhile the seaside had disappeared getting replaced by overall rocky hills rising up between fields of sand. Every now and then a huge advertisement board would pop up on the roadside showing a mobile telephone or a food product. Sitting in the third row I naturally had a good view out the front window. So far, I payed attention to world outside. Suddenly my heart wanted to come out of my mouth as two sand colour army tanks came into view blocking the road ahead of us. Feeling slightly choked I pushed back into my seat. Our bus came to a halt and heads and bodies pushed into the aisle behind me to look what was causing our stop. A minute later a handful of soldiers in sandy uniforms bearing Bordeaux red coloured berets entered in the front of the bus and began to demand documents from the first row of passengers. Everyone including the soldiers were quiet. I looked as unimpressed as possible and luckily the leading soldier peered into the remote part of the bus swaying his face from one side to the other and after returning calmly the documents to the occupants of the second row he commanded the soldiers behind him to turn around and leave the bus. Surprised and very relieved, I had already seen myself being asked to retreat with them from the bus because of my foreign passport, my heart manoeuvred itself back into place and struck up the song *your in the army now*.

Passing the tanks we slowly moved and anticipating that Cairo must be near I asked my seat neighbour if Cairo lay in short distance. He nodded without saying a word. On one side of the road a high brick wall came into sight and continued along the highway for miles. Every now and then watch towers appeared in the wall overlooking metal plated gates. Directly I thought of the military apparatus. Soon more and more vehicles filled the roads beside us and along the road's buildings appeared growing in size. I knew Cairo was home to 20 million people and I had experienced Bogota, its equivalent but there the buildings were mostly smaller but none the less endless. Sporadically our bus stopped to let people off. I knew this meant that if the bus was passing through the area of your destination you could ask for it to stop. And most likely Cairo had a couple of main avenues leading inwards connecting the different districts and areas. So, I thought it would be sensible to tell the co-driver that my intention was to end up in Agouza.

He signalled to me to me that he understood and we left it at him telling me when it was best for me to get off. Looking through the window I saw motion everywhere. Black haired men and boys and occasionally female heads trapped in colourful cloths. Here and there cows and goats and horses came into view tinkering along close to the pavement. The co-driver caught my attention, so I made my way towards the front of the bus. He pointed at some taxis which lined a colourful and chaotic vivid looking pavement with an institution like building behind it. Down the steps of the bus I went approaching a monotonous level of different noises. The bus had halted just for my sake which made me nervous having to nimbly collect my luggage from the bosom of the big waiting vehicle amongst passing people and motorcycles.

What made me most nervous was that I couldn't speak a word of the local language and this amongst a backdrop of hectic. How was I supposed to react if I got approached by rowdy men who had registered my alien arrival and sought to relieve me of my big western rucksack. Having shouldered my rucksack and bayed farewell to my assistant I stepped onto the pavement amidst a clangourous noise with the traffic horn the most prominent one heard out of all. Up to a rolled down window of a taxi I stepped and I grabbed the attention of the young man behind the stirring wheel. He looked at me. I looked at him and pointed at a word I had written in my notebook. "Yes, Agouza please." He nodded ushered me inside where I quickly placed my rucksack on the backseat next to me. The heat was on in the city, the sun slowly descending and this man pressed on the acceleration peddle to rarely let it regain its prime position. I couldn't make out any traffic rules except the constant use of the car horn. We sped fast and furiously across flyovers, searched for gaps in traffic to press on through to maintain our speed and out over the Nile we shot turning right at the end of the bridge where he smoothed into a further flow of traffic. Shortly afterwards a left was indicated and after questioning some pedestrians the taxi driver stopped outside a high rise in a densely built and populated area. A dusty bush lined the pavement with some trees towering amidst it. We had arrived at my required address. Shortly afterwards a small thin woman with strawberry red lips in her sixties appeared clapping her hands in front of her chest displaying a face of disbelief that I had arrived. I payed the driver and turned to greet the elderly grey blonde-haired woman with three cheekbone kisses. It seemed to me appropriate because she was swiss. She was quite astonished to see that I had arrived most convenient and without further notifications which normally occurred due to difficulties getting from A to B in this huge and chaotic city. Into the building we stepped under the close eye of a handful of middle-aged men who were standing around everywhere in the entrance hall.

The building had a concierge and somewhat fourteen or so floors. By now sweat was on me and excitement within me. She lived on the top floor which at the same time was the roofs finishing floor and on it was a wooden shelled bungalow amongst many head high plants. Cairo's buildings were all around us in a light screen of smog and the boisterous voices of the Muezzin cut the air but I couldn't make out from which surrounding mosque or pray tower it echoed. The call to evening prayer was aloud. Lisa welcomed me warmly to her home, showed me the guestroom and I won an overall nice impression of her dwelling which displayed a cultivated cosmopolitan pan euro-oriental touch. I much thought I would feel at peace here in her home.

CHAPTER 6

After I installed myself in my room, Lisa and I sat down in her cosy resting part on the roof terrace to eat a variety of snacks. She had prepared hummus, olives, cubes of Greek cheese and other small mediterranean dishes which we ate with flat airy white bread. Red wine, cigarettes and introducing tales and descriptions of one another's life accompanied the delicious little feast.

Every now and then as I looked out into the distance, past Lisa's withered and with mascara belayed face on through the branches, did my eyes and mind rest and gaze at the concrete skyline with millions of windows pipping through clouds of smog. Very wise and beautiful was Lisa to place or nearly stuff the terrace with tall and bulging plants and blossoming flowers which had a soothing affect against the otherwise overwhelming tone of endless grey either in concrete or the air. Slowly a quintet of fighter planes emerged into view flying low and trailing colourful smoke behind them. Some what struck I asked Lisa what was going on. The military were adding a bit of a show to the current situation was her short reply. The aircrafts drifted slowly out of sight over the endless horizon of rooftops.

We returned to telling each other parts of our lives what we were doing for a living and why we both had come to Cairo. Lisa on the one hand had left her birthplace Switzerland due to complications which arose out of the narrow mindedness of swiss society and the indulgence of the law into private matters. I am referring to family ties that get challenged once the outer world begins to change and the individual with it. But to which consent and in what kind of conformity. Conventions got renewed and a majority flocked around them whilst the dispatched sought refuge in distanced anonymity or buddled themselves into the depth of their solemn and sanctuary interests. Which of course was feasible both home and abroad. The great question aloft and dying for resolvement was how to meet and make means to maintain a home for oneself.

Lisa had been fortunate to bear a son but his inter-weavement with dubious people after adolescence and the coupling with the same sex had brought him early death with surrounding difficulties for her to clarify why? These circumstances visual to me bore weight on her being which left her in a fragile and slim body frame. She pulled on her cigarette at a fairly high cadence as she resembled her distant impressions of her past life. My telling of myself had similarities to her but I of course was much younger as I had to adopt and find a way around Berne, Switzerland under the weight of the dispersion of my beloved Irish family, which led to the early death of my father. Maybe at this point our common path began to get trodden upon. She became curator of a respected gallery in Cairo and I began to express myself with colours. On informing her that I worked privately with colours she introduced a be-friended artist of hers to me and sure enough shortly afterwards the man himself appeared. His name was Hesham. He had short curly brown hair, looked a bit yellow and fe-verish, hadn't shaved for a couple of days and to our surprise because he hadn't given it away at first sight, he lifted his dark suit trouser leg to grievously display his swollen and infected foot and ankle. It looked terrible and even more horrible was the obvious that being out and about in a filthy city without a bandage wasn't supportive, probably because proper medical treatment cost too much and that him conferring to the treatment with painkillers was the most, he could do for himself in this moment. Lisa tried to intervene but he wouldn't accept any advise on the matter and he assured that he had his cure by his own means and ways. Not long after his arrival he invited me to come and visit his home and family. Hesham is in his forties and his dwelling is more or less close by to Lisa's. During our conversation I noticed Lisa striking a hard and sincere cord of tone whilst talking with him which left me feeling double warned and she told me to stay aware around him. Plainly he was the artist boarding on the verge of self-destruction. He looked it and I had seen it in others on my various encounters with artists across the world. I agreed to accompany him knowing that the plunge into local life was about to begin.

As we left the building night had fallen and people nearby paused to observe us as we made our way through the neighbourhood. Walking at a steady pace we crossed street after street with more pedestrians about than vehicles. Then we passed through a shanty town where I wouldn't dare go hadn't I been with him. But to the truly impoverished foundations of the place it was also the most artistically decorated quarter filled with beautiful garlands and the traditional Ramadan lanterns. The local children were interested in us as we strode through but naturally, I left the talking to Isham. Moving onwards we eventually came to halt in front of an originally beige coloured building but over the years black soot and pollution additionally made up its outer appearance. It was another high non impressive building of flats. In we went where he knocked on the first door on the ground floor. A couple of moments past by and an elderly white-haired woman opened the door slowly to see who had knocked. I was hushed in promptly by Hesham and heartfully welcomed by the woman who was his mother. I told her briefly my name and where I came from to then lose her attention because a boney arched nosed semi bald headed man with spectacles sitting half way down his nose appeared in the doorway in the middle of the corridor. He glanced curiously at us while Hesham bayed me to come along. The walls and the ceiling were completely covered in black cobwebs. Slightly stiff from surprise I followed him accompanied by a very hairy cat. Behind the door where the thin man had been standing sat four men in total on two beds paying the most attention to a small television box. Hashish smoke filled the room and whilst one was smoking another was occupied with rolling the next hashish joint. The window shutters were closed, but the window was kept open. Two bed lamps gave a dim light to the dark and cobweb covered room which otherwise housed a table a cupboard and the item that made me feel the most comfortable was a nicely woven beige carpet covering the floor.

After introducing myself and on their inquiry, I told them my main interest for being in town. On saying so, I didn't get much of a reply set aside Hosni Mubarak and his scoundrels self-beneficial corrupted system which had been replaced by the fraud voted into presidency Mohamed Morsi from the muslim brotherhood. I asked why he was saying "fraud" because I thought it would be quite difficult to rigid an analogically done vote with a population the size of Egypt. The man then told me that the ink in the used pens at the polling stations had self-erased and the papers were there-for clear for fresh assignment with proper ink. That way of describing a fraud vote could be plausible because I knew of counter ink pens but it didn't seem very likeable to me because why would the corrupt powers want Morsi? I didn't see the muslim brotherhood organisation very capitalistic orientated. The sharia law which they may have wanted to erect step by step doesn't put markets first. But in comparison with reality it benefits the biggest capital holders in a sharia organised country. And from what I had read in newspapers quite a lot of international observers had been present at the time of the vote and reported that more over things had been done proper democratic giving Egypt its first national vote.

Secondly a population deprived of equal wealth flocks naturally around them who nourish them and give them spiritual support. I wouldn't say a revolution happened because a small part of the population was impoverished and disillusioned obviously and very much bluntly it was the other way around which so very often is the case which leads to the toppling of the head of that minority which had been exploiting regardless. I mention the head of the body had been battered and to this very moment the body was still operating in form of air force fly over shows here in Cairo and rebuked military presence at strategic points. The body remained functionable but as the world could observe the new head wasn't fitting very well at all. The body had all the powers supported by even stronger external powers that wished to set the people into movement. Most likely a very difficult task for the new head to surpass lingering powers within as well as surrounding ones with their well organised instruments to give the voting majority what he had promised in turn for the individual vote.

The four men turn the subject towards their existence which merely I wouldn't have guessed from either of them, besides that they were all family members of a sort.

One was a director of something, the other a lawyer whilst Hesham's two brothers worked temporarily on oil drilling stations out in the desert and at sea but at the moment labour had dried up for the two of them. The thin bony fellow dragged hard on the hashish joint and conversed rapidly into some sort of a fit which shook him vigorously to a lying position on the bed. It looked crazy enough but the men reassured me that it unfortunately happened regularly to him.

The two higher educated men left obliged to return at some stage reminding themselves and us that they had elsewhere other commitments to fulfil.

On their retreat Hesham began to tell the story of his noble father who had been recognised by the sultan as an architect and painter. Great projects had been accomplished by him which were still visible in form of a mosque for instance but as like some stories in life go the parents separated and a decline began to set in in the life of the siblings and their mother. Hours past, his brother recuperated, joints of hashish burned down to the stud, TV show after TV show covering Egyptian events past through the screen till finally I had enough and had to break the bonds of the moment to demand the possibility of going outside. Only Hesham agreed so soon we left the peculiar apartment to stroll the night streets and chat some more. After Isham had bought from a street vendor a number of medical tablets which activated his nerves to the equal of the drug *speed*, he was hard to catch up with and to starch to persuade to sit down for a glass of tea along side the road to watch the world go by. Although it was well past midnight life was very much vibrant everywhere we went. Businesses were open maybe all night long. Cairo might well be the equivalent to New York, where as New York does sleep a bit more.

At last after numerous attempts Hesham agreed to sit down for a tea. Listening to him whilst I drunk my hot mint sugar tea his forehead and temples beamed constantly from the layer of erupting sweat. He told me lots of stories out of his life that gave me an insight into his caste of people and Egypt's way of dealing with children, youth, man and woman, religious pluralism, carrier developments, corruption, generally said the different types of perspectives a person can hope for whilst growing up. A lot sounded quite unbelievable to me. When our teas were finished, we picked up our previous pace and on we legged it again. We walked remarkably fast which was quite straining. Going along I observed his swollen dark blue ankle with open wounds stepping along in front of me and all seemed crazy. Endless streets with endless shops and no change was in sight. Any sort of professional medical attention which I repeatedly proposed to him wasn't on his mind. Another couple of hours past and eventually we crossed the wide slow flowing Nile on a bridge to emerge onto the scarcely populated Tahrir square which lay in white strongly illuminated under many bright floodlights.

In the centre of the square camping tents stood erected and many banners hung on them with anti-Morsi and anti-military information. People sat about engaged in quiet conversation. The square didn't appear to me as big and vast as it looked on television during the huge demonstrations last Sunday when people had gathered insisting Morsi's retreat. The number of participants counted by official sites estimated 17 million people that day. On the face of one of the big buildings overlooking the square one could see the positions of the television broadcasters occupying nearly every single balcony with their turned off tilted cameras.

There were hundreds of them and each crew had its

on little box. It looked very similar to the inside of an opera house. We crossed the square and entered a web of narrow streets and passages which were lined with small tea and coffee parlours. We were in the area the intellectuals frequented during the first and the current peoples uprising. The area at this late hour was lightly populated but still everything was open. We sat down sipped on our hot sweet mint teas, relaxed our legs, puffed our lungs and sat more or less in silence. I had been hoping for a lively round of debate and exchange on how such a mobilisation of people was organised and maintained over months of combat with Hosni Mubarak employees. Isham couldn't come up with a meaningful answer. I changed the topic to my current love affair which I wasn't sure if I meant it as much as I thought I should do. Funny enough Hesham didn't have any great answers or ways to handle my situation but instead he led me out of the tea parlour maze to a man who called himself a doctor. He welcomed us in to his ground floor apartment told me I could ask him what ever I liked because he knew the answer to everything. How promising I thought to myself as I examined this neatly dressed heavy elderly man blessed with a balled head left with a little bit of black hair on its side. So, my question for him was, after I had explained to him my current state of affairs with the woman, if I really loved her? Within myself I wanted to feel more intensity towards her but it didn't exist how I imagined it should do.

The doctor for everything simply repeated the question so that I had to respond. My answer after juggling the question amongst my breath and brain back and forth and from my belly to my heart up and down was simply, yes I do. Well there you go, he replied plainly. So that was it. A phrase spoken for a future with her. On top she was embedded in a situation I imagined would be prosperous for myself if I came across it in life and I had come across it in the form of her and the situation was attached to her.

I thanked Dr. Osman and back into the lamppost lit night streets we emerged to arrive home with dawn breaking shortly before six in the morning. Much exhausted I lay myself into bed and most instantly fell asleep.

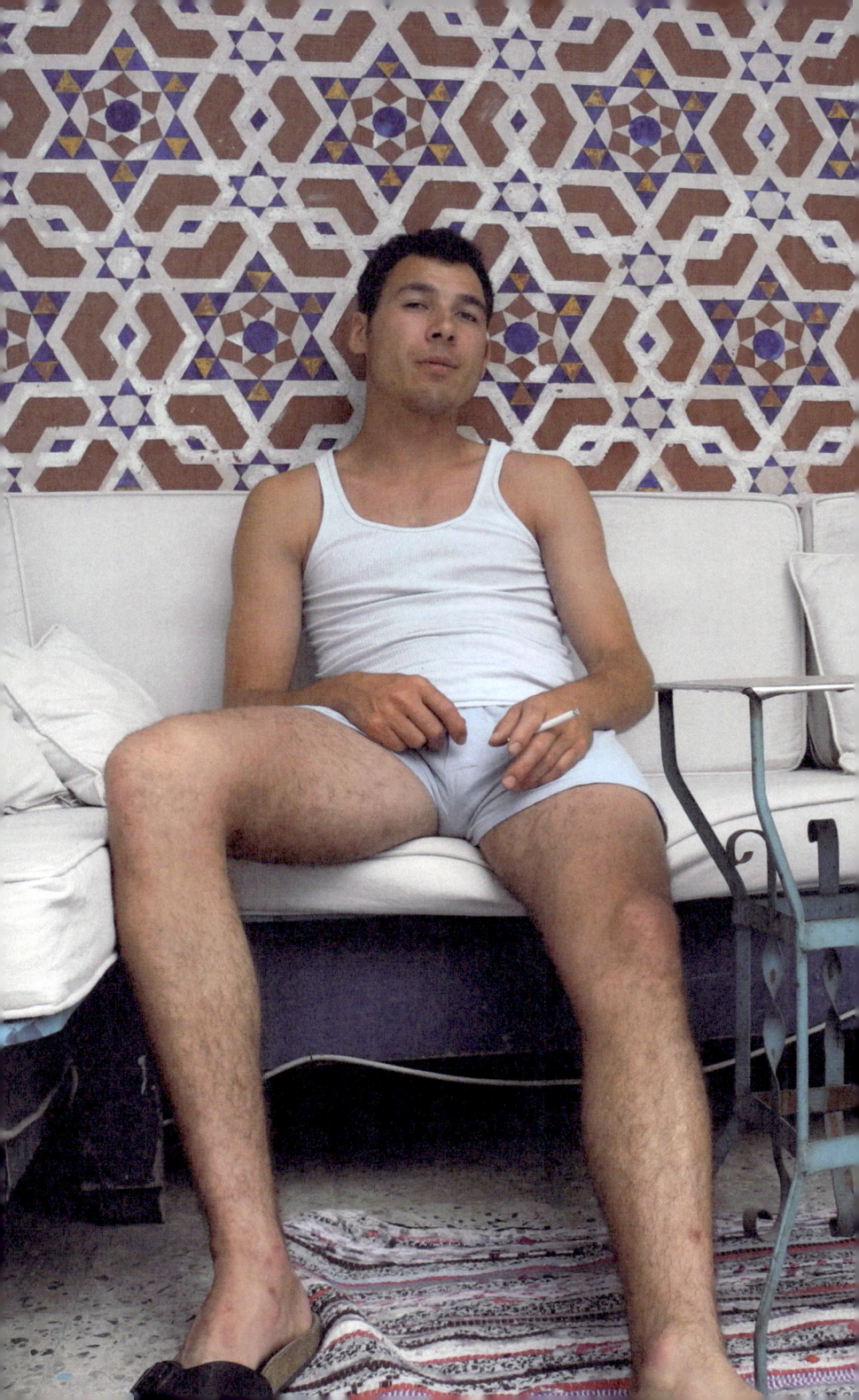

CHAPTER 7

The first I noticed as I reopened my eyes was that I felt quite sticky. My body was covered in sweat and while I arose from my mattress, I thought it would be pretty had to cool myself down, because as I looked my clock, it was close to mid-day. My brain ached slightly and I wondered how I could do myself some pleasure. After a reasonable cold shower while drying I straight away began to sweat again, I went to the kitchen thinking of pleasure in the form of food. Lisa didn't appear anywhere on my way through the flat, so I assumed I was alone. The best I could do for myself was to make a tomato onion omelette, which certainly helped me revigorated my state. After having ate my lunch I circulated a bit on the rooftop staring into the city trying to figure out what sort of life happened in the buildings. On the rooftop of our neighbouring building I could observe a large family with many children going about their ways because most of their living space was in plain air and only covered by a canvas. The interior underneath the canvas was laid out like in an indoor living space. Gaining such an open view it brought me to realise that they most likely were the family of the building's receptionist or concierge because in a book of Nagib Machfus, he described exactly what I was looking at. It seemed to me as to be quite a good place for living due to the overall natural ventilation or it just did look appeasing as I compared it to living inside Isham's apartment or myself waking up in a room this morning covered in sweat. Also due to the distance and the lower position of their rooftop did I feel a bit like a giant overlooking the little people placed on a tower platform scurrying back and forth amusing themselves, whilst they laughed and shouted at each other. The city lay to my feet and looked all so much softer and acceptable seeing it in it's existence the other way around.

Back inside it took me a couple of moments to dress up in a common male fashion and soon after, I was back in the streets searching for a shop. Lisa had left me a note on the kitchen sideboard with a small description on where I had to go to buy some bottles of red wine for the evening dinner. The shop was located on the Nile island of Zamalek which lay opposite to our neighbourhood Agouza. Up onto the bridge and down the middle of the island was way to go. It should be quite easy to find also because it was the only shop selling bottles of wine for miles. Wearing shirt and trousers I left our block noticing the 30°degrees plus heading for the Nile which flowed parallel to our quarter with the twelve-lane road on it's side. Once I reached the big road, I could see well in distance the bridge leading into Zamalek. I crossed the road dodging cars and mini buses so I could pick up transportation for a short while in the right direction. Having reached the other side, I stood amongst a small group of waiting people and stuck my arm out to help stop the next approaching mini-van. We boarded a small Toyota van and I knew the bus couldn't go anywhere else but straight for the distance I wanted to travel and the cost would arise a soon as wanted to get off. Sitting amongst daily life I discreetly looked at what surrounded me and when I hopped off after handing over my coins to the co-driver, I was happy to have begun my search conveniently. Zamalek appeared to be a wealthy neighbourhood

118

consisting of higher quality buildings and more green spaces in between.

I think I even saw a cricket lawn. And by the number of security employees standing around building entrances the whole appearance of the area seemed clear to me. Life was much scarcer here, so I didn't have to fear getting stopped by people looking for contact for which ever reasons they ever had. Which would have been street vendors, beggars or people wanting to talk to me because they had noticed I was a foreigner or there was always the possibility of getting robbed. My anxiety came from not being able to speak the local language. Seeing that anyway hardly any citizens were about there wasn't really any point in worrying. After walking straight ahead for a good while, I reached the described flyover with the cumulation of shops beneath it and one of them was supposed to have wine.

The place wasn't allowed to advertise on its outer shell that it sold alcohol but to know its name and location was enough.

The place inside appeared non-extravagant and was small. I was handed the desired bottles in a plain one coloured bag without any brand or emblem on its sides. But while halting for a brake and a tea close by and on my way back, I did feel I wasn't the only person knowing what was inside my one coloured plastic bag. The looks I received seemed a bit unusual.

The sun scorched relentlessly upon everything below it baking stone and life as it guarded its place or moved along.

Later that evening Lisa cooked chicken liver with lyonese potatoes accompanied by steamed broccoli. The bottles of red wine were warmly recieved by her guests which had amounted to me, Hesham and a frenchman who worked for a transnational company which produced potatoe chrisps. He was involved in the flavour creation department. Dinner tasted very nice, the wine was well tempered showing its strong substance with every gulp I took. Our table conversation included all of us and centred mainly around local developing events.

Lisa was more or less content that Mr. Morsi would have to make up a new future for himself because for many secular orientated people in the country, did the muslim brotherhood pose a threat to their way of life. The frenchman sided with Lisa in the anxiety of a radicalizing brotherhood if they should further be able to hold on to power. I think Isham saw his liberties at risk equally but feared the brotherhoods reaction if Mr.Morsi really did get toppled in coup d'etat. He knew that the brotherhood made up a great part of the egyptian nation and thought that many held fire arms in their homes. The mention that every family in the counutry had a member in the military services seemed to me a key fact, meaning that the members position as a stable income for the family was vital and had the potenial to balance the mediocre satisfation towards the egyptian state. None the less we would know in an hour or so.

Prime time television held the channel with the precise information for us and the world, with the military and their associates in the producers box.

At eleven o'clock, we had the television on, general Abdel al-Sisi, wearing a big pear of sunglasses declared the ultimatum for Mr.Morsi as expired and noted that the people had wished him to step aside. Having not recieved any resignation from Mr.Morsi in the meantime , would he and his fellow generals cancel his presidentcy and transide power into their hands. Him general Abdel al-sisi would be interim president till fresh elections were shedueled in a couple of months. He further resembled the citizens to guard their calm and draw back from any violent reactions to the militarys imediate decision.

Looking at eachother and especially at Hesham because he was our main translator nothing was instantly said. Eruptions of noise filled space and time circulating us completly. A multiple tone roar swayed through the concrete valleys alighting into the air around us maintaing itself for several minutes. Out onto the terracce we carefully stepped to be confronted by a night sky freckled with many colours.

The blasts from fireworks replaced the vocal noise and continued for at least twenty minutes. Next door someone was shooting illuminated ammunition into the sky which was destinctable because of its linear green lines. Well, all in all what a sight was created above the roofs of Cairo. As far as one could see just bouquets of firework lights. The television commentator proclaimed that 17 million people had gathered in places throughout the city and one especially familiar place was packed to its outer walls. The Tahrir square was the centre of the jubilant people and I asked Hesham to go out with me. He agreed but first we went to his families flat where we met his mother and brothers. She seemed pleased but the men were eager for hashish. We had to wait a while till the product arrived.

In the meantime I slipped an envelope full of egyptian pound notes to the men's mother while I visited the toilet. Lisa knew the brothers wouldn't use it for what she wanted it to be used and had instructed me to pass it secretly to their mother because otherwise the cash probaly would have decreased before it would have landed in her hands. In other words, Hesham or his brothers weren't to be trusted with money. At the meal table Lisa had told me enough stories of him squandering his earnings on intoxicativ products. He was a gifted artist and painter and through Lisa he was able to sell some of his productions. I think his excessive habits interfered with his organisational capabilities leaving Lisa feeling obliged to help him in fullfilling the final requirments of a project of his.

So after numerous requests from me for us to leave the flat and the hashish we set out into the night to find vibrantly filled streets with the egyptian national flag wrapped around many a person. The nations colours also appeared painted on peoples faces and everyone was in good spirits. Men and women aswell as children were all taking part in a night stroll but the one thing that kept me not fully included, was the notion that I still hadn't a clue what they were talking about. Which words did they use to express their point of joy? How did they explain their hopes and thoughts of what was to come and what was to be done? I really couldn't interact.

Hesham had even told me not to talk if anyone asked me anything. How could I respond, I didn't know a word properly and I think the least spoke another language than arabic. Normally I would reply to someone asking something off me. It's difficult not too. But for some reason Isham thought it best for me to withhold my forgein personality. Up till now walking amongst crowded roads full of people nobody had asked us anything and we probally didn't look like aliens. Especially not Isham and for myself I again had tried to dress as commonly as possible. Long trousers and a dark long sleeved cotton linen shirt. On my feet I wore black leather one strapped Birkenstock sandals.

For myself I was quite content with my dress-up. The temperature had lightly reduced itself but still the heat sweltered around 28°degrees.

Arriving at one of the bridges crossing the river Nile, we were greeted by a muscular man standing on a big lion statue which formed the bridges head waving an egyptian flag and making the victory finger sign. His face was covered by the white Zoro mask from the movie "Anonymous". Passing people willingly wanted to pose with him for a photograph. While crossing the bridge one instantly noticed the drop of temperature coming from the strong constant cool gush of wind arising from the Nile's water route. People stood lined along the railing of the bridge embracing the refreshment. It was a real relievement walking across the bridge and we took our time while I eagerly observed the people. A real proper natural air conditioner. Down on the narrow stone embankment next to a busy road lines of white, yellow and red plastic chairs were set up. Mainly turtling couples slightly restrained from one another occupied the seats while glancing at the glittering night water iluminated by bright city lights. On the water long colourfully lit up boats moved about giving the impression of floating discos. And every now and then away in the dark sky a bouquet of colourful light drops rained down and vanished. At the end of the bridge a short distance apart from the towering lions military personal in khaki uniforms were stationed next to the road standing around their rubber wheeled armoured tank vehicule. They stood by watching and posed if asked by pedestrians for a photograph. A constant flow of people past inbetween the bridge railings and in the middle of the road waited a man sitting onboard his old horse drawn open black wooden carriage hoping to attract customers and exaggerate the already special moment in everyone present life. Further down the wide boulevard now flanked by tall thin pine trees we arrived at a round about with a big shallow white stoned water fountain in its middle. Again astonished by the scene, the same coloured plastic chairs were set up around the fountain with couples holding hands and glancing from their companies face into the water and back.

Or they just stared patiently at the water and the fountains water jets. Here it even occured more clear to me that the people were really observing the falling drops of water and the sparkle the reflecting over head streetlights created on the water surface and within the single water drop. The foam created by the arriving water jets on the water surface seemed worthwhile looking at aswell. Somewhat struck by the barreness of the simplicity in this spectacular scene I could clearly recognise the romance it withheld for the observing lovers in the otherwise fancyless enviorment. I poised several moments engulfing the scene and pointed out the originality to Hesham. He smiled gently saying nothing.

Every now and then when seeing a scene portraying the instant moment would I descreetly shoot a photo. Then suddenly while walking on the boulevard again, a young man stopped to face Isham talking vigorously. The fellow was about twenty five years old and a couple of seconds later he turned towards me asking in a persistent tone if I was a muslim. I held his questioning glare without moving my lips. Isham responded for me and willingly I cooperated with him and we both turned away from the questioning man to move on. It was a strange moment and a sticky question depending on the mans intentions. On the left side of the road rembrants of ancient egyptian culture appeared infront of the national museum and close by the red star of the city's metro transport service signaled an entrance to the underground system. Space around us began to get crammed as we reached the outer railings of the Tahrir square. The space ahead of us was a sea of colourful headed people overlooked on one side by hundreds of lights from the recording television cameras placed on the balconies above the square. The people chanted loud and clear "Horai ah masri" constantly while they waved their flags. I joined in the chorus. Sporadicly a firework exploded high above our heads which provoked an outcry of joy.

Me and Isham stood still. Suddenly the whole quare went silent. Everyone poised and glanced struck by something which no body could see.

I instantly thought of the long stick swinging camel riders who on previous demonstrations had viciously attacked people in the name of support for Hosni Mubarak.

Hesham had told me that they were the camel owners who gave guided tours to tourists at the pyramids of Gizeh. Still dumb struck the crowd swayed from left to right boarding on the verge of a mass panic stricken run. Thankfully the crained heads eased back onto the shoulders and nothing happend but never the less Isham wished to leave. Crossing the packed square I took photos of specially happy scenes. In one part of the square we came across a mini van carrying a television crew on its roof filming the celebrating people who followed behind as it ploughed slowly through the crowd. The television commentator had changed into an joy animator. Close by an elderly face beaten bearded man in a grey jalaba was pushed and dragged along by a group of people. It wasn't clear what had got him in such a state and situation. Then another man came into view fallling from the night sky dressed in a snow white uniform shedding a smile acorss the onlooking crowd. People below him had got hold of him and were throwing him up and down in joy. Dangerously near a howling car engine could be heard and as I cautiously stepped closer a red low key race car came into view spinning round and round in a circle with the co-driver sitting on the windowsill close from being flung out into the clapping and flabbergasted onlookers. One mistake and people were going to get killed if the driver lost control over his vehicle. We continued our walk and the howling engine noise slowly faded out of earshot. We had reached the narrow alleys and streets where the tea and coffee parlours were situated. Small groups of men and women sat close to one and other deepend in discussion. We too took up chairs in their verse and ordered tea for our brake. I wondered if the people were discussing their next moves or what had to be proclaimed now that Mr.Morsi was dispatched from power. Had they weighed their opportunities and possibilities now that the military was their compatriot or was the military their opponent? I had seen people holding placards with pictures of general Gamal al Nasser and the present general Abdel al Sissi on them. Some obviously layed hope in the military bringing balanced and people orientated solutions for the country.

A handful of western males were also present in the the narrow passage way involved in the group discussions. Was their a common vision for the revolution after this evenings events? I didn't know. From what happend in the following months I don't think there was a strong idea that challenged the military and it associates. But certainly not favorable was the fact that al sissi exercised a strong censorship throughout the information outlets and everyone who literally spoke out critical or non-approving of his ideas and suggestions got demonised by state and hyper-private meaning capitalist media companys into fear of repression and imprisonment. Which became the case for many a vocalist of true popular change for Egypts society.

Life in Egypt slid unstoppable back into pre Morsi times without any opposing outcry from western states who were allies of the people during the revolutionary days.

Meanwhile Hesham had led me away from the tea parlours and we were walking through downtown Cairo. The buildings were built in french style architecture and pointing a finger from a banner strung up across the street Usama Hussein Barack Obama, president of the United states of America, looked determind down into the street. Written below him was the information that he and the USA supported terrorism. Surprised of what I saw I took a photograph, then turned away to face the red with the white cross Swiss hostel sign stuck up over a door in the massive building next to us. Was Hesham showing me this on purpose? We continued our walk. The air was now solemly filled with heat and only vaguely could one hear a distance away the echos of the megapolis. The buildings had meanwhile shrunk in size and the streets were quiet and deserted. We had entered a Villa neighborhood with tall fat palm trees towering above locked in behind walls and metal bar fences. No wind blew. Suddenly Isham halted next to a vintage car and called out to me to take photographs. I hesitated first, then asked him what I should photograph? He bluntly answered, "me", patted his arms put his shirt in his trousers and refastend his waistbelt.

Now I understood lightly irritated by his instant exposition in front of the old car. He posed by the cars bonet then leaned against the wall, sat to its foot, stretched his arm out and I willingly pressed the button of my camera numerous times. The street was filled up with orange light from lampposts and was favorable for the photoshooting. In the distance I could make out the al-Nasser tower behind Isham. Quietly a ginger haired cat appeared between the high metal bars and jumped down from the wall. The cat pranced slowly towards Isham curled itself around his legs and pressed tight against them while looking at me and the camera.

CHAPTER 8

The following morning after a late breakfast and a resummeration of the evening and its events to Lisa, I made my way back to the Tahrir square wondering what it would look like after the celebration. I kept my clothing common and beneath my arm on elbow hight tucked well in my small dark blue cotton sidebag which got absorbed perfectly by my dark blue linen shirt I carried my quality camera. I had bought it specially for this trip and was lucky to have got it for a very good price because it had been the shops window sales model and now it was meeting its purpose. Down in the buildings entrance hall as I stepped out of the elevator and walked past the waiting people I could feel the concierges and his surrounding companions alert eyes rest on me. I greeted estimating that I could and should move freely leaving the building steadily postured. First I wanted travel by Metro and have a look at what I came across for graffitti reasons.

Painting the Metro train was another reason I combined with my visit to Cairo and today seemed to be the right moment to engage in a bit of sneefing about for that purpose. Down through our quarter beneath Dokki street lay the closest Metro station. Having made it onto a train, I don't remember if I bought a ticket or not, I was quite happy to be underway. Thinking the ride would be simliar to Paris or New York I stood in my place by the door expecting nothing. But all of a sudden two young men in their early twenties standing in front of me began to harass and molest a woman their age standing next to them. Shocked by their behavior and their aggression I looked around to see what the other passengers were thinking or intending to do. No one in the relatively full carriage seemed willing to interfer. Overall trying to keep a unnoticed and non-forigen position for my own safety, I diverted the thought of taking up action because the two chaps did leave an insane impression on me as I deboarded at the next station. It was Cairo University. Leaving the station I thought I would resurface in a friendly environment.

Having no clue of anything really, the signs didn't tell me much, I stepped out onto the street and walked along for a bit. There were lots people about. Again my surroundings didn't appease me at all because swiftly the place was turning into a trash dump with horrible dark greenish patches of water in front of the heaps of rubbish. The colour of the water looked deadly toxic and wouldn't let me see to it's bottom. Slowly I felt I was beginning to panic. I hadn't an idea where I exactly was, feared my position of looking and searching about being lost which could lead to me being confronted by someone. Groups of ragged children were playing about in the street and the adults who were close by the buildings seemed to be shouting. Not knowing where to go I saw myself becoming a light target for robbers and eventually ending up in one of those horrible water holes. Strongly rejecting such a situation I turned on my heels and went straight back to the Metro station. I boarded the next train and disembarked at Tahrir square. My anxitey had reduced itself to a cautious state of alert as I resurfaced on the brim of the square.

Not many people were present on the square in comparison to the night before. Now in the centre of the square could I see a tent site with many placards and egyptian flags erected. Seeing that among the tents a gallery like exposition was installed I headed towards it. Information and drawings where placed on paper boards and even some sculptures belonged to the collection.

I took my time in inspecting the display. Everything shown had to do with the egyptian revolution that had begun in 2011. I took some photos and walked on towards high buildings on the squares rim. The balconies with the television camera teams were meanwhile scarcly occupied. Though to one side of the building below the balconies a large group of women mostly wearing the headscarf had gathered and were chanting and shouting slogans in choir. Men stood about as onlookers or joined in the chanting. Having a good view from where I was standing big mural paintings caught my eye which covered up all the walls surrounding the square. I began my walk at the beginning of the first mural and went through all that I could see in convinient distance. The content of the paintings displayed the events that lead up till today and had formed the peoples uprising. One mural was for the 54 people killed in Port Said during or after a football game. Others showed the police violence the people had to endure. Some showed the imperialism Egypt was embedded in and other related to the muslim brotherhood. Overall I think none of the pictures or drawings would have found there way into the outlet of mainstream media although they were all very well painted. The murals were the peoples mediation of the events. A form of speech which certainly wouldn't have been tolerated during Mubaraks regime and most likely isn't tolerated today under the current dictator. I felt quite overwelmed looking at some of the paintings and by the fact that they portrayed and reclaimed free speech under very violent circumstances. After inspecting all the paintings that I could come across I returned to the square. Now I saw a bald headed white man dressed in a light blue shirt holding a microphone and looking into a television camera which was being lead backwards in front of him and he was following through a crowd of people. I recognised the man as the live news comentator for Sky News. Realising that if I would go up close behind him, which I obviously could, literally stand behind him and wave with both arms, like people in the stands do when a football player is taking a throw-in on the side line of the pitch, maybe my aunt in England would see me later on in the news show on Sky television. Thinking to myself that it would be immensly funny I walked up to him and did it for a minute or so. "Look a white boy enjoying himself in a serious situation. Later back home in Switzerland I went through that days Sky News show on the companys internet site and found the sequence from that moment but the producers had cut me out. Shortly after his coverage of the Tahrir square a police helicopter flew into the middle of the square and hovered above our heads for at least twenty minutes. Then it flew out among the buildings and away. Following minutes later a rumble close by in the sky began to brew and suddenly five fighter jets raced across the clear blue evening sky letting loose trails of smoke in the colours of the egyptian flag. The crowd below first poised then began to shout and roar in excitment. Shortly after the planes first overflight they returned and drew a heart with their trailing smoke high above our crained heads. The people went crazy. How strange I thought, the military drawing hearts when they actually kill love. None the less a lot of people were very happy and celebrated franticly. I shot my photographs, looked around myself once more, joined in the passionate choir and chant with the people in will to fulfill "horai ah masri". Then I began to make my way home to report the militarys interaction in the days event.

Once seated in one of Lisa's cosy terrace sofa chairs I began to describe what I had seen on my walk about across and around the square. While we were talking the fighter planes returned to the cloudless blue sky reproducing their smokey air show. Lisa explained that through such actions the egyptian people could be easily convinced that the militarys support was genuine for the common good. Meanwhile big helicopters had also arisen to the sky and were hovering slowly over the city's roofs.

The impression Lisa was giving me, was that she wasn't very touched by the events. As if they wouldn't affect her much. Her prime interest was not to be in Switzerland while secondly she gave deepend interest into individual destinies.

Later that evening she invited me out to dinner. The restaurantwe went to was located on the very end of Zamalek Island and from our table seat we could see the water of the Nile being split in two. As we took up our white cushion seats dusk simultanously paced onwards aswell as the water did around us. The city's skyline background was exchanging yellows and oranges amongst a ever growing dark purple while the barges on the Nile turned their direction as they reached the head of the island. Music and laughter swayed across the glossy unrippled water surface and everything left me feeling very lucky and grateful. Around us the people presented themselves in a extremely western fashion and not a single vale was knotted around a womans chin. I was astonished to see how beautiful these egyptian women could be once the long covering garments were lifted. All in all everything I knew seemed very far away.

During our meal Lisa and I opened our personal cupboards and shared events out of our pasts. I wouldn't have thought a big farmhouse close by to where I once lived outside of Berne which I knew from seeing was her childhood domicile. But on the other hand she was familiar with my aunts and their young lives of her time. It was still the same in Berne.

Today our families were still meeting eachother in the same places but in following generations. Her nephew was a friend of mine and the woman I was engaged with his cousin. So far, I didn't miss any of them. No one I knew had shared an interest in political altercations or the combats people had led to achieve the change. The food that we were served was very well prepared, seasoned and cooked but the most remarkable was the restaurants hoummus.

The answer I recieved for my inquiry why it was so delicatly smooth, was that the peel of every single chickpea got removed by hand. Well it certainly made the difference to the hoummus I had come across till this evening.

Meanwhile a further bit down the Nile a big procession of Morsi supporters was crossing the 6.October bridge searching for access to the Tahrir square. Unfortunatly they were met by a large group of opponents and fierce violence broke out. The two fractions battled relentlessly with eachother summing up a new death toll. Now foreign involvment seemed even more displaced to me and seeing the simliarities in the participants I wouldn't have figured out by myself who belonged to which party. There wasn't even police or military present during the ongoing clashes whiched raised questions the following day. The authorities had let them wage war on eachother. The Morsi supporters were wondering where their democraticly won election had gone and was going. Their gatherings were growing by the hour around the Muslim university and Naser City. Simultanously the military were stepping up their presence and establishing their superiority in who had the say in the city.

For the country's people it ment they were drifting apart. A division was taking place and the military were stepping out of the shadow to present one of their own to the people as a possible democratical elect whilst the Mubarak structures remained firmly concealed in the dark. The military even had the say in who could candidate or not beside them. Meaning they chose their opponent.

Isham who I met the following day didn't disguise his anxiety and seemed even more agitated than elsewise. Being worried to the bone he told me to accompany him to one of the local mosques where we should engage in prayer with the other men. To me I thought it would be interesting to witness ongoing muslim life in a mosque. Once inside the buildings hall we took off our shoes.

Apparently the mosque had been designed by Heshams father. In the main prayer room I placed myself on one of the plastic chairs set against one of the numerous pillars holding the ceiling. The inside of the mosque was very large and all across the floor carpets were laid out. The interior was made completly of white stone and I think the floor was of total white marble as well.

The walls included high long white tainted windows which illuminated the spacious room sufficiently. In the front of the room opposite the entrance a three step pulpit stood for the prayer leader. Thinking I wasn't aloud to join in their rituals I sat in my chair looking forward to observe the show. A good couple of dozen men were present and sitting sided along eachother barefooted on the floor. The Imam dressed in a long robe entered the room from a side door and mounted the three steps of his pulpit. Everyone in the room stood up. Suddenly a man called to me to join in the line.

I didn't see any possible excuse for me not joining in or else I would have to leave the room. So more or less joyful I placed myself next to the inviter and followed the physical movements of the line. Up and down we went. "Allah akbar, Allah akbar" and other sentences were said where I just mumbled along. Afterwards when the last movment and chant was fulfilled we faced eachother crosswise and shook firmly eachothers hands as far as one could reach around oneself. Walking through the streets afterwards with Hesham, he got greeted every now and then, he told me that it was a sensible move we had made in visiting the mosque. Many muslimbrothers lived in the neighborhood and through our engaging in prayer he showed himself on common ground although he actually hardly ever went to prayer. Repeating that many of them held arms in their homes and after the outburst of violence one couldn't know who would lose his calm in this hot situation. But during this sensitive time in Cairo it obviously felt adequate to him. For myself I wished to see the pyramids of Gizeh but Hesham told me that it was highly unrecommendable.

I shouldn't even go out by myself was his advice. Literally, I began to feel stuck and if the violence would spiral out of control maybe I wouldn't even make it across one of the bridges which led to the airport. I dreaded a military curfew. My mind began to look for an exit although my return flight was still two weeks away.

CHAPTER 9

Another evening began in the company of the three brothers and a cousin with glasses of sweet mint tea and hashish
cigarettes. We were spread out across the two beds and
one chair. Isham's brothers dozed deeply mixing up the
hashish with pharmaceutical medicaments. The two men
close to their forties were strongly addicted and their bodies and faces displayed the toll. Both were thin, yellowish
pale and narrow faced with one of them wearing small
wired spectacles. The two continuosly told me tales of
themselves adding on questions which I wasn't always able
or capable of answering. My impression grew that they
actually didn't have anybody else to tell what they were
telling me due to the social codes and conditions of egyptian life. Their stories were very tragic and very personal
and they went so far that one of the brothers ended in a
having an epileptic fit. The fellow foamed out of his mouth,
shook meanly, went up and down on the bed while his
brothers and cousin explained to me one just had to let it
happen till he physically calmed down. I asked to be allowed to wet some cloths which I intended to place on his
forehead and neck. The man didn't notice much what was
happening around him and how we stretched him out on
the bed. One thing I had noticed in the build up to his fit
was that the brothers kind of subtly brawled with eachother in who was aloud to speak to me. Lisa had notified me

that the brothers had servere jealousy issues. Their hissing and verbal shoving at one another did seem a bit more than a normal conversation and I anyway didn't understand a word they said. Sometimes I even found it difficult to find a phrase to bring their irritating monologues to an end. It had grew challenging for me to let them speak on and on just out of politness. Obviously they had things on their hearts which through me found a receiver. The three of them went so far to agree that I was one of them. Simply said a brother of theirs. I couldn't understand why exactly but I supposed it had to do with my listening and the way I balanced their speaking time.

Or did they have a spirituality I wasn't aware of ? Them leaving all the insects in the apartment to share the space with them and their mother did have something mystical about it. Their mother was very present and alert for her old age and on top she lived with her three sons and seven cats. From their tales of her marriage to their father who was in the circle of the late king of Egypt something non-usual must have been within her.

The following day past very simliar except a muslim-brother I had got to know told me not to leave the neighborhood because it was seemingly too dangerous. I stuck to the local cafes. As dusk set in Lisa handed me before I was leaving to visit the brothers another envelope filled with banknotes. This time they were from a friend of hers who knew the family as well. Again I was asked to pass it on discreetly to the mother. This evening no change had alternated the sweltering heat that kept its tight grip on the city. The air was filled with the many voices of prayer from the muezzins which glided into one another spreading a blanket of one overall humming sound. I was quite sure Isham would be at home and not in one of the local mosques neither his brothers. The streets I past through were lightly frequented. Having knocked on the door and poising my ear to listen if I could figure out any noise from within the door, it was opened slowly by the mother of the house bearing a big smile.

She beckoned me in with an arm gesture and then faced me and lent forward with her head to cheekbone kiss me. I immediately responded and gave her two or three kisses on her cheekbone and inquired how she was. Looking down the corridor Isham poked his head out of one of the rooms and was startled by what he saw. Instantly his pointing finger went to his neck and he slowly pulled it across his throat. Wondering what I had done wrong I brushed his gesture aside telling myself his mother had insisted on the greeting style, so he would have to back off. None the less, it left an uneasy feeling in me. He withdrew back into the room and I seized the moment to pass on the envelope with the cash to his mother. Leaving her behind I found the men seated in their places and everything looked more or less as evenings before. One change did occure to me that the running television hadn't any pictures of protesting people to show but instead only wafflers in shiny grey suits with ties babbling away at one another in a studio acting as if their speeches were of great importance. Besides the joints we smoked the two thin boney brothers competed with eachother till they began to hiss at one another in who claimed more of my attention. The developments of the last 48 hours were grinding me where I sat. Everything seemed unbelievably cruel and incredibly alien to me. I wasn't aware that life on this planet could look like it was where I were. Blunt and mellow existence in a unevolving environment erected within invisible walls which kept people distant from their nature and probally always a step short from one anothers touch of joy. Lisa had told me Isham had agreed to participate in a competition of Fenuz designing, so I was very relieved and glad as he stood up and bayed me to follow him to his room and working space. Entering his room the next shock set in. The wall beneath his window was knocked out and the rubble lay heaped in the open gap. Several cats instantly stood up and purred for attention from Isham as he stepped inside. I had to mind my step everywhere I trod. The sight of dwelling reminded me very much of a friend of mine back in Switzerland.

The Fenuz is a lantern which gets installed in the period of ramadan. Normally the shell protecting the flame of the candle gets illustrated with pictures out of peoples daily lives. Truely Ishams Fenuz extinguished everything around it once I fixed it with my eye. His lantern shell was made of glass window pains and on it he had drawn colourful pictures with an enhancing type of see through colour. It was roughly over a meter in height and broad in its cask. Simliar to an old London gas lit lanternpost. It looked beautiful but wasn't quite finished yet. His time for accomplishing was on Tuesday which was two days away as was my newly booked flight to Athens.

During the previous day after I had explained to my distant love and girlfriend how things were going she proposed to meet me in Athens. She could organise her getaway from her dental studio as quick as I could from Cairo. She really threw a rope to pull me out of the hot sand. Not having to think intensly about her suggestion I booked the flightly via Internet and let myself wind up her rope. Her idea withheld a small apartment for us on Paros one of Greeces many islands which we would reach by ferry from Piräus in Athens.

Isham settled down to continue his work on his fenuz and I asked him for a blank sheet of paper to draw on. We both sunk into our doings and the cats retrieved to their resting places or left the room via the gap in the wall. A couple of peaceful hours past by with his brothers pooking their heads through the doorway. The room was never the less still warm and filled with stuffy air. The picture I drew with crayon colours was my graffitti name placed on the Cairo metro train just as it was leaving a station. I hadn't succeded to do it in reality so at least I could imagine it as a picture and Hesham could have it as a present. Once finished I told him he could have it. He was grateful but I don't think he understood what the initial intention behind the picture and what actually graffitti was. He responded by showing me some of his paintings which he had in his room. After looking through them he eventually wanted to present me with a couple of them.

Seeing that these paintings could attribute to his finacial income I offered on return all the egyptian pounds I had on me. They amounted to a 170. One painting showed cats another army tanks in a populated town withholding egyptian flags while the one I liked the most was a unfinished painting in black and white of a vintage car and a donkey with a cart. Leaving his room shortly afterwards to rejoin his smoking brothers in front of the television I felt happy having bought local contemporay art. Back in front of the television I figured out relatively quick that I couldn't remain to long because the nonsense that Adel was spitting and mumbling up didn't occur to me. It made me feel nervous and restless. I gently arose, thanked Hesham who had meanwhile also rejoined us from his lattern painting and wished all a peaceful night. Back in Lisa's flat I showered cold and embraced the coolness spreading in my body for the time being. Strangely enough I wasn't able to find sleep straight away. It was past four o'clock in the morning and dawn was shoving the nights darkness slowly through the concrete towers and valleys of the city. Suddenly loud bird chatter began to fill the air directly infront of my window. A bunch of birds chatted briskly amongst one another rearing the memory of an old roman saying, that when birds sung so early in the morning, on the verge of dawn, it withheld the message of death. Startled by the thought and the memory of Hesham crossing his throat at me I sincerly wondered what lay ahead for me. Sweat began to pearl from my body as I turned from left to right and back again under my bed sheet.

Waking up around midday feeling moist and sticky in my room I arose out of bed rather swiftly and revigorated. The bed sheet laying next to me, had lost it's purpose shortly before I had fell asleep. Leaving my room I headed directly for the kitchen where I found Lisa pacing up and down the room pulling heavily on a cigarette.Straight away I wondered what was wrong with her. Looking at her and the way she covered her face with too much make-up, it was her normal way of doing it, but it still looked strange in the heat and I couldn't understand why she did it. I don't think she was trying to cover her wrinkly face with the adjusted amount because it certainly wasn't working. Seeing me step into the room she directly approached me and asked me if I had heard the news? I denied any contact with a radio or television since I had gone to bed, so I asked her to inform me. She nervously looked aside and then with a touch of tristess portrayed what had happend earlier on in the morninng in Nasr city. At least fifty people had been shot and killed by military personal. The soldiers had opened fire on a crowd with the intention to disperse them. Later on television claimed a man had withdrawn a wooden rifle at the site and the security force had reacted on his behalf. But why shoot fifty people if one person held an old pellet rifle. In succsession the muslim brotherhood had called for it's supporters to revolt against the military presence in the city which of course cast a new atmosphere of paralysation over the city. After listening to her during our following talking pause I directly began to worry if I could make it across the Nile once a proper armed conflict broke out seeing the airport as a potential battle ground. If such a situation would unfold I might have to leave for the airport 24 hours in advance of my departing flight. Well how exact was the birds message and their sing had took place parallel to the early morning massacre. During my lunch we discussed the possible outcomes and Lisa was convinced that the military would maintain control over the city.

After washing up my dishes I felt like going for a walk. I guided myself within our neighborhood till I longed for a seat and a glass of hot sweet mint tea. Life around remained in place. Elderly women wearing headscarfs drew their donkey and carts belaiden with vegetables through the calm street, shaking their hand bells. The shoe cleaners young and old found their customers along the tea parlours completing their service in a vigorous and skilled manner releasing their customer properly neat. In the shade of trees, walls and buildings mechanics with their kit spread out on the ground went about their job under the keen eyes of the onlooking owners of cars or motorcycles. The horrible scenes of weapon violence seemed far away and even slightly unreal. The tea service lads greeted me friendly and inquired if I was fine which I couldn't deny. Later on I returned to my local family.

I won't produce their surname for reasons concerning their safety. Back indoors infront of the telly the evening played out simliar to the ones before. Only this evening my level of reception was lower than on previous nights, so I politely baid farewell to return to Lisa's rooftop flat in search of my bed. So far things had stayed calm throughout the city.

Due to the various reasons for my early departure which I would have had to explain did I decide not to inform the three brothers. I had won the impression that their strong affection for me would have created a very awkward situation for myself while sitting and explaining in the middle of their family den. Feeling kind of guilty for my options I didn't want to arouse jealousy and experience it's awfulness. So, I kept my promiseful retreat plan to Athens to myself. On the otherhand or in my second heart I still wasn't feeling love the way I wished too or thought I should feel it for Karine in my absence from her but all in all the thought of a reunion with her soothed my heart and mindaches. Considering my whole wonderful issue I might have felt unsure of her reasons for wanting to be with me. A corn of disbelief lay inside me suggesting that it was close to unbelieveable that a woman like her should genuinely love me. She had never told me proper reasons why she shaught my person and I didn't really see any common grounds between us. Everything she related to was new to me and everything I did was distant to her. The result was I only moaned to my mother about the differences between me and her but at the present moment I wasn't even aware of such sentiment. She wanted to come to Athens I wanted to get away from Cairo. Blunty said, I couldn't come up with anything better for the rest of my summer holidays. Practicly it meant I had to change sail to manage the new course starting gradually now.

Spending another relaxed day and night in Cairo departing again early from the brothers and their mother I now sipped on my last glass of hot sweet mint tea. I informed the service lads of my dispatchel from the area and as I made baid farewell to them we cheekbone kissed and exchanged firelighters. Lisa called a taxi for me which arrived shortly after her call. Saying goodbye to her infront of her block of flats I thanked her gratefully for everything she helped involve me in. We reminded eachother to remeet in Switzerland in the premises of her sister and nephew. Once a year she went to visit them. We cheekbone kissed farewell maintaining posture while the taxi driver loaded my black and blue Mammut rucksack into the booth of the car. Mounting the taxi in the co-drivers seat I felt relieved to make my departure from an adventure which had unfolded so much different from how my imagination had primarily erected what would lay ahead for me. I waved to Lisa and her onlooking neighbors. The taxi driver drove at a reasonable speed as we passed the places that had become familiar to me. The bridges crossing the Nile were open and on our way I saw burnt out buildings left in their torched state from the time of the first revolution in 2011. Military tanks were in position along the roads without causing any interruption to the flow of traffic. The square in Nasr city where the massacre had taken place lay soley occupied by a handful soldiers and their vehicules as we past heading towards the flyovers leading through the valleys of concrete.

On entering the airport building I was greeted by a nervous man in his snow white uniform accompanied by a colleague in a dark blue one. They straight away ordered me to hand over my luggage and stand still while having to stretch out my arms for body inspection. My luggage was placed in a scan machine while the officer in white ramped through my pockets pulling out everything that lay within rudely informing me that I wouldn't need the money anymore. Feeling uneasy I just only realised minutes later that the man had openly robbed me of my money. His behaviour was desperate and yes I wouldn't need the egyptian pounds in Greece.

But such action from a policeman showed me how helpless and vulnerable an encounter with them could play out. I'm not quite sure if the chap even took my cigarettes off me saying smoking was forbidden in the airport.

Questions weren't directed at me about my time spent in Egypt and I was just happy to collect my baggage and leave the brut behind to fulfill the aeroplane boarding procedures. Back in the sky I baid farewell to the overall sandy colour beneath which gave way to a sparkling dark blue below and a light blue with a white fringe around me.

Down there lay the Mediterranean sea I told myself but with shores that were very distant to the ones I knew.

CHAPTER 10

The flight to Athens past easily with me mainly reminisc-
ing on what I had experienced in Egypt. Overall I felt relieved but again also guilty being able to change shores
without any complications. Putting it in another picture it
was like changing the television channel. Fed up with what
I had seen and hoping for satisfaction through new enter-
tainment. Leaving the gates of Athens airport I stepped
out of the metro train at Omonia square. In a side street
behind the square I had a year earlier come across a low
star hotel asking for 15 euros a night. The room was tidy
and the beds were covered with clean white sheets. An old
thin tall man in his seventies or eighties ran the place. A
small balcony overlooked the street below. The following
morning Karine was due to arrive and to me a funny idea
had arisen within me. All I had to do now was to search for
a big enough piece of cardboad or if lucky an equally sized
piece of white paper. Both objects were easily recovered
thanks to the piles of waste piled on the streets curbs waiting for the rubbish collecters. Back in my hotel room I began to fill my time with the creation of my idea which I
then would complete at Karine's arrival in the airport hall.
I wanted to make a welcome placard for her to then display it outside the sliding exit doors of the baggage claim
section amongst the onwaiting crowd and other sign holders in the arrival hall. The text on the placard would read:

Tschiki, welcome under my wings.

I was using the name Tschiki because she had primiarly come up with Tschiku for me. In swiss german language a U at the end of a name indicates a male bearer and an I at its end a female. So my reaction fitted perfectly to her name creation. Originally the word is spanish, *chico-chica* for boy or girl.

The following day dawned rather quick and I began to feel nervous and curious for her perception of myself. I also wondered if our emotions for one another on meeting again would glue our lips together and if our arms would hold tight what they just had got hold of. Plus was it possible that ripples of human electric would run through us tuneing our senses for as quick as possible sex? I had experienced these feelings with my first teenage girlfriend but I also honestly had too acknowledge as I walked along the street back to the metro station that the pull or phisycal draw towards Karine wasn't that intense.

At the airport I took up position between the men wearing buisness suits holding small placards bearing the name or company of the expected person. My placard was six times their size and I hoped it would be unmissable when she walked through the sliding exit doors. I was well on time, so I lingered, keeping an eye on the sliding doors while letting my gaze glide ocaissionally across the hall observing the emotions and actions ot the other waiting people. The airport was busy and buzzing.

The information screens told me that her plane had landed, so it couldn't take much longer from me wrapping my arms around her if she wanted me too. Inwardly I first hoped that she would read my sign and then run to me delighted. Time past, the doors slid open hords of people emerged without Karine's cute face amidst them. The doors closed again. Moments of mutal joy arose on some faces of encounters. Stern reliefment and plain gratitude on others. Where is Karine, where is my Tschiki . But still I felt like an alien waiting for an appointment that required my reasonable participation.

Then at last inbetween a variation of faces her beautiful image appeared searching for mine. Her light brown hair was tied behind her head and like usuall she left a straight fringe line across her forehead. She was dressed simple wearing ladies shorts and a olive green silk top with lowcut old school baseball shoes. On her back she carried a coloured hiking rucksack. She saw me I saw her and pointed towards the placard I was holding above my head. She raised her eyes but before she fully had read it she was in my arms and our warm fleshy lips traced eachothers loosening to cross the cheekbones, kissing on around the eyes, one two times on eachothers forehead gently to then return back to the lips for another couple of seconds. We released our grip to look at eachother. I smiled broadly she blushed returning a soft smile. Welcome to Greece, Tschiki! Her response to my placard was a short laugh. Nothing more was added. It became quickly a burden for me. No feeling of sexual longing erupted within me. Off we go Tschicki! But a feeling of uncertainy began to unfold in me as I thought of her having to stay in that very basic and simplistic hotelroom. The woman could be acustomed to better but at least it was clean and price worthy. I took her rucksack and she carried her handbag obviously showing signs of caution. My placard found its resting place tilted next to an airport bin.

Later on that evening as we took up seats at a rooftop table in the heart of Athens for dinner we only slowly got into casual conversation. Sofar no accusations where brought up against the hotelroom which was relieving for me. On the other hand she did show much intrest in my recent time spent in Egypt. Poising shortly to think what I was going to tell her I inwardly felt ashamed realising that a lot of my time was spent smoking pot with the brothers. But it also showed me that more wasn't to be expected off them because it was mainly their way of life. I had done the best I could under the given circumstances. I can't remember me having anything to tell her that would have opened up common ground between us except my waving at the television camera from behind the news reporter. Moreover I felt mind blank and found it inappropriate to let her know. I was thinking more about how and what I should communicate with her than expressing my feelings. Truely I think I wasn't even capable of defining them. Maybe being back in Europe and amongst its attitude of everything is fine, irritated me into a state lacking coherrence. Finally having a well sheltered woman infront of me brought me to the limits of my capability, as a man at that time in life. My kind of being contradicted her kind of being and that left me experiencing insecruity around her.

We dinned and shared eachothers pleasure for our discovered dinner location on the top of a high building observing the setting sun as it shed its colour spectacle across the endless rooftops below us which at least arose both our senses for romance. The night was hot and sticky without us supplementing further ignition. Our room had two seperated beds.

The next day we left Athens by speed ferry boat to take up lodge on the barren Island of Paros. Karine had organised a small but sweet two floor apartment in the heart of the white washed town. Unfortunatly my thoughts continously circulated around the question: Do I love her or do I not? Hardly any other relieving and comforting ideas or alone thoughts were effective in casting my mental array aside. Poor woman was the bottom line of my mind carousel as I began to imagine that she must be noticing my disconection towards her. I even expected a question or two from her but nothing alike crossed her full lips. We led a pampered holiday life with her birthday marking the middle of our vacation. During the day we undertook outtings together to remote beaches which we accessed with the help of fishermen offering their small boats for service. As we went about setting ourselves on the lonely white sanded shores a common pleasure did emerge between us. She aswell as myself appreciated a bit of nudicity and textile free swimming in the deep azul blue sea.

At one point as we took our lengths I ended up entangled inside her with nowhere to stand on. My arms rode the surrounding water while my body rocked simultaneously with the waves. We both felt delighted but soon our shared ease disolved into exhaustion and then we had to give it up because there was nothing there to carry us. Cherishing life we retreated to shallow waters to prolong our initial deep sea manouver in a small rock bassion filled with sun heated water. People were still in sight on the horizon and as visitors in a foreign country we kept ourselves ducked and paced our moves slowly intending to avoid an outcry from co-islanders. The collective return voyage by boat to the main port of Paros still lay ahead of us on the embers of the day.

Karine's birthday dawned and on beforehand I had prepared a floral wreath with a candle in its middle on our breakfast table. Outside our apartment a pink and white nerium tree blossomed powerfully over the narrow white alleyway which made my search for flowers easy to fullfil my soothing and festive birthday decoration present. I can't remember exactly the main present I had purchased for her but I think as we arrivied back in the town from our remote beach I told her some excuse so I could distant myself from her to look for most likely a moderate piece of jewellery. I honestly valued and respected her but my constant buggering and bothering question of "where is the love?" for her had to get dealt with. Saddly enough was it her birthday but better tell her my feelings than feel supressed and continuously irritated. I hoped that the core of my action would result in a peaceful state of mind including even some sort of sober conversation regarding our relationship. After the semi joyful breakfast, she had appreciated the wreath, we set out once again insearch of a remote hot sandy beach. This time we rented a motor-scooter and I drove us half round the island along dusty pothole scattered roads till we arrived at a long stretched sand beach with a couple of sturdy trees on one side. The strand was deserted and the short trees provided the savoring spots of shade.

We agreed to settle down and I urged myself not to hold back my will to free speech any longer. Thinking it had to be done sooner than later I stretched out my hand to her just after we had unloaded our bags containg our beach gear and took hers.

I drew her closer to myself telling her I had something to say that was weighing me down, which she might have noticed by now. Inwardly I trembled but the longing for my hope helped me steady myself. She looked at me straight with a genuine touch of interested innocence.

The brilliant sun in the cloudless sky poised directly above us. Too late now shot through my head and out came the fatal words describing feelings which needed clarification. I basicly repeated to her what I had told Doctor Omar back in Cairo. Why was I wondering what I was missing in my relationship with her? My love for her didn't feel as strong as I wished it would and I ended with, "it had to be said". She stood straight and poised for a second letting loose an expression of disbelief flash across her face. She responded directly asking if it was nescesary being her birthday. She turned away from me looking disconcerted and sad while the wind picked up her hair as she began to walk slowly along the line of breaking waves on the shore. Agony arose within me as I realised what I had just done. Standing with a brow of sweat in the hot sand, empty handed, my gaze fixed her parting back then swayed out to sea in search of solutions for reparation arising on the horizon. I waded into the water to halt as I felt it cover my kneecaps.

CLOSING EXTENSION

For the rest of our holiday we were able to get along with eachother. I tried to make physical contact with her but without success. Towards the end of our stay we were capable of smiling at eachother. We flew back sitting in seperate rows on the more or less empty aeroplane. After a month or two we got back together again which lasted for 10 more months. Our relationship didn't really gain more depth but we none the less had nice times.

After numerous attepts to give up smoking cannabis I experienced multiple times simliar conditions and states of mind as I went through with Karine in Greece. The distress the addiction created within me while distancing myself from it only came to my realisation after multiple achivements where I could retrospect and acknowledge the connections. At the time neither me nor Karine sensed that disconnecting from cannabis could create such awkwardness. She never really smoked the drug herself.

Settling back into the town where I lived after the summer holiday I was encouraged to write a summary of my experience in Cairo and then send it to the local newspaper. I agreed on doing so thinking that there should be genuine interest on behalf of the newspaper seeing that I was providing first hand coverage of the events that had taken place. I didn't even recieve a word in response from them.

The general enthusiasm on behalf of all the western media outlets which had accompanied the coverage of the various uprisings across north Africa quickly turned cold and no support was expressed for the reassurance that the progress these people's assemblies had sought for was actually followed up on and implemented in the new constitustions by the newly installed goverments. The initially supportive western States vocalised no accountabilty towards the succesive forces in power.

Another result of the wide coverage of the promising events was that the political content created ever so much hope for change amongst people claiming the values and the state of being on an individual level evolving from the words and meaning of democracy, sovereignty, independence, freedom and inclusion. But somehow a lack of contribution towards the implementation of the overall acknowledged words in the first world manifested itself in the actions of the co-powers and their true intentions came newspaper article after newspaper article into light. Military rule established itself bringing forth the following democratic elected body who was himslf from the military apparatus. The International Monetory Fund rolled out their support scemes plunging the recieving states into huge finacial depths attaching delusive hopes for general prosperity. Big buisness and the so called markets recieved primarily attention while the narrowing of the people's horizons and possibilities followed as the logical outcome of a culture benefiting financial maximized profit. State protectionism got proclaimed and nearly all states obeyed and began quitely to arrange. This meant the already established in states alternated their finance structures and governance systems to strenghten the effort in defending what they already had. Weakend or another word, instabil north Africa fell pray to the first worlds war industry which ploughed fields in search and hope of possibly reaping in new profits through their experienced exploitation practises. Back home austerity programs had been running since the great finacial swap in 2008 which had worn people down through their daily enviorments. Such as for the majority of people mainly being the work place. The work force additionally had been enlarged by the inclusion of more women while their children came under care through commercial daycare centres operated by generally poorly educated people but financed by the state or private capital. State instistutions were equally included in the austerity programs and subduced to less funding which resulted in people seeking their support after their broken illusions the media had previously helped create which then failed to materialise due to dynamic policies were factually incapable of recieving appropiate and quality support adjusted to their individual needs.

Health disturbing and mentally grinding waitinglists resulted. Boarders were beginning to be centred in the media picture and in reality extra fortified where they had already softly existed. A side effect of the policy, boarders in peoples mind and in their behavior. The people of the world discharged from their original plots by these first world scemes began to move in search of inclusion into the societies assumably functioning on the allover acknowledged words which I need not repeat. They were leaving their own societies due to their forced exclusion on the base of unfulfilled promises their uprisings couldn't maintain and realise. Space for them in the IMF scemes was scarce and what was leftover by the new goverments was reserved for their associates and family members. Simply said, the already rich were on the recieving end and it was looked upon them by the giving rich to maintain a new state of stability for the alined buisnesses of the providers.

To succeed the continuous establishing of digitalism was spread throughout the first world which concentrated and created a state of being focused on superficial topics. Mostly regarding one's own person. Reconaissance and education began to wither as a result and the heads of state could begin to publish their policies in one sentence on messeger platforms tapped to the internet.

Meanwhile back in Eygpt I have unfortunatly learnt that the original death toll from the various massacres carried out by the military in Nasr city and on precisely the square I had past by arose to pressumably 2000 and more people. Never in modern world history had in a single day so many protesters been liquidated as had been on Rabaa square. They had resulted from four or five single events in Juli and August 2013. The eygptian state offically denounced these facts. The first democraticly elected president Mohammed Morsi perished in a Cairo courtroom while on trial. He had ever since been inprisoned and unlawfully treated since his ousting. His predecesor Hosni Mubarak lived to undergo a process of rehabilitation. The USA presented the eygptian state with 4 billion Dollars intended for the military. Sadly also the whole embankment running along the river Nile in central Cairo which I have described has recieved reconstructed and people are only aloud to frequent it in return for a fee. The Tahrir square equally has been reconstructed with the aim to prevent people from gathering for extended periods of time. Public places have been commercialised while the general city citizens financial income is reduced. And now in 2023 a new war as began in the region with strong support from the first world and everyone is distracted from their legitimate claim to personal prosperity.

Exsiting military structures included in states are false guarantees of preservence to the acknowledged words that withhold the hope of sane life amongst people and towards their co-livingbeings of this world.

The only liberation for all from these scemes of subjugation is probally to be found in the reduction of economic production and in the sharing of the already existing. A development of self-independence combined with social emancipation within society supported through the connection with nature and its rhytm would benefit the search for liberation and the true fulfilment of the acknowledged words.

23.03.2015 Rathausgasse, Berne

A day to our departing. You respond to his shy stroke on your arm with a searching clinch upon him as he's giving way. Swelling courage within your departure. Belief in your sprawl for Mr.Wright. Your lips conceal a furtherous Odysseus to that believed state. How nice to see but helpless dangling, hangs the heart in my breast, believe'n in the same.

Special thanks to Lisa, Isham, Karine and Boris
for designing this book

Horaia masri